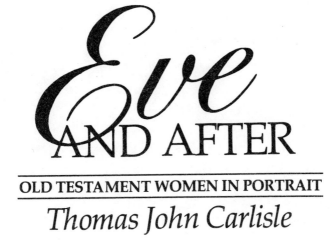

Eve AND AFTER

OLD TESTAMENT WOMEN IN PORTRAIT

Thomas John Carlisle

GRAND RAPIDS

William B. Eerdmans Publishing Company

Library of Congress Cataloging in Publication Data

Carlisle, Thomas John.
    Eve and after.

    1. Women in the Bible — Poetry.   I. Title.
PS3553.A73E8   1984   813'.54   84-1551

ISBN 0-8028-1970-2

ACKNOWLEDGMENTS_____

The author wishes to thank the following publications, in whose pages certain of these poems first appeared, for permission to include them in this book: *Christian Century,* "One Good Quality," reprinted from the June 1, 1983 issue, copyright © by the Christian Century Foundation; *Christian Science Monitor,* "Emily Dickinson," copyright © 1961 by the Christian Science Publishing Society; and *Alive Now!, American Weave, Christian Education: Shared Approaches — Reform and Recovery, Church Management — The Clergy Journal, Concern, Enquiry, Gospel Herald, Immaculatan, New York Times, Presbyterian Life, Purpose, Response, Rotarian, Saturday Review, Time of Singing.*

A number of these poems have been copyrighted by the author prior to the publication of this book. Some of these poems have also appeared in books of poetry the author has published previously: *Celebration!, Journey with Job,* and *You! Jonah!*

"Rise Up, My Love, My Fair One" has been published by Shawnee Press as a choir anthem and as a solo set to music by Dr. Arthur W. Frackenpohl, who has also set "The Daughters of Zelophehad" to music.

PREFACE _____

The women of this book remind me of another woman who was ahead of her time: Emily Dickinson. I have written this poem for her:

> The daffodil she sent to me
> arrived a century late.
> The calling card she smuggled in
> lies on my hallway plate
> while through my residence resounds
> the tiptoe of delight:
> the woman with the perfect word
> demure as dynamite.

The description "demure as dynamite" is true of this outstanding American poet who lived in the nineteenth century. It is also true — but in a great variety of ways — of most of the biblical women of this collection. They had a certain singularity. They were not stereotypes. They were not inferior, even though their culture at times seemed to work against them and so imply. They were real people. They made remarkable contributions. They were indeed *demure as dynamite.*

These poems describe most of the fascinating women of the Hebrew Bible. I have provided Bible references for many of the poems so that you can easily look up the passages referred to and be reminded of the supreme artistry and significance of the original — and decide for yourself whether I have been reasonably faithful to the biblical account.

It is my hope that through these poems these dynamic women may speak for themselves — to you as they have to me. Although they lived many centuries ago, they still can amaze us today, can enrich and bless and inspire the lives of men and women alike.

This book is dedicated to my wife, Dorothy Mae Carlisle, who is also demure as dynamite.

v

APPRECIATION_____

I am grateful to far more people than I can name who have given me encouragement and specific insights. Among them are Dr. George M. Landes and Dr. Phyllis Trible, professors at my alma mater, Union Theological Seminary in New York City; Dr. Katharine Sakenfeld and Dr. Jack Cooper at Princeton Theological Seminary; Dr. John C. Purdy, who first commissioned me to write poetry based on the book of Ruth for an adult Bible study; Prof. Joan Donovan of St. Lawrence University, as well as other associates in our Presbytery of Northern New York, including Rev. John B. Smiley; Janet Harbison Penfield, Mary Seth, and Mary Ann Gehres, associate editors of *Presbyterian Life;* Dr. Barbara Withers, Rev. Gail A. Ricciuti, Dr. Patricia Kepler, Dr. Keith Crim, and Rev. Jeanne Audrey Powers; my sister, Elizabeth Carlisle Lewis; our sons, Rev. Dr. Christopher Davis Carlisle, Rev. David L.H. Carlisle, Rev. Jonathan T. Carlisle, and Thomas Dwight Carlisle; and, most persistently and patiently, my beloved wife Dorothy.

My mother, Ruby Grace Mann Carlisle, and my father, Thomas Houston Carlisle, encouraged me to write poetry from early childhood onward; Prof. Samuel Allen of Williams College encouraged me in my student years. In my experience at Union Theological Seminary, of incalculable importance to me was the inspiration of Dr. Julius Bewer, my Old Testament professor, and Dr. Mary Ely Lyman, whose enthusiasm for the Bible was contagious.

Indispensable to this book coming to fruition in its present form is my editor, Mary Hietbrink.

To all these and to many, many more I am forever grateful. Part of the joy of preparing *Eve and After* has been the enthusiasm and solicitude of so many friends, named and unnamed, who I hope will accept my gratitude.

THOMAS JOHN CARLISLE

CONTENTS

Study Guide   109

FOREWORD

At first glance the Old Testament gives every evidence of being male-oriented. Men are full-fledged people, whereas women are most often treated as inferior. Women are worth less or worthless. Sons are urgently desired but daughters are not in demand. This orientation is part of a patriarchal society. The authors of the biblical record are men — and only men. What chance do women have in such a book? No wonder some contemporary women feel that they must find a new faith, a different religion, because the Old Testament seems so heavily weighted against them.

How, then, is it possible to write a book of poems about women of the Old Testament if they are so systematically excluded and denigrated?

The fact of the matter is that despite their culture, despite their society, despite the masculine authorship and authority of the Bible, the genius of God shines through. We must remember that we in our day understand God only partially. We too are greatly influenced by our culture. We too have been terribly slow to recognize what we may now call self-evident truths.

One amazing thing is that this male-oriented book includes a number of feminine metaphors for God — although even modern male translators often effectively obscure them for us. And some women seem perfectly happy that they should do so.

Inevitably the biblical accounts mention women. Usually, however, it is not considered important to give us their names, though men's names are almost always recorded. Many a significant person is merely listed as someone's wife, someone's mother, or someone's daughter, or is identified as a woman residing in a certain town or city. Given the Hebrew emphasis on the importance of a name, how could these women ever surmount such a major obstacle? It was difficult, but they did and they do.

Male pulpiteers have perhaps unconsciously omitted employing Old Testament women in their texts and their sermons. When they have used these women as examples, they have tended to emphasize what are considered to be their negative qualities. So Eve becomes a warning and a shame rather than an inspiration. Jezebel is a favorite target because it is easy not to recognize whatever good qualities she may have had. Job's wife is automatically maligned — out of context. Sarah is blamed for Abraham's errors. Even Bathsheba has at times been branded a shameless hussy!

When women have been praised, it has been primarily for child-bearing (actually for son-bearing!), for submissive obedience, for giving their husbands the credit for their own accomplishments.

All this indicates an obtuseness on our part regarding the Scriptures — a blindness, a deafness, a perverse unwillingness to see what is really there. We need to realize that if the male authors include the affirmative action of as many women as they do, there must have been many more women who are not mentioned but who must have made significant contributions. We know this to be true for all of recorded human history, including our American history. Ignoring this fact can scarcely be excused as benign neglect!

The male authors tend to downplay or disregard the injustices forced upon women — Dinah, for example, in Genesis 34, Jephthah's daughter in Judges 11, the Levite's concubine in Judges 19, Tamar in II Samuel 13. Yet these women speak to us nonetheless — if we will read the Bible with open minds and hearts. Although the historian does not clearly offer a compassionate judgment in the recounting of the story of David's daughter Tamar, when we read the story for ourselves we are struck by the magnificence of literary presentation, which penetrates our feelings and responses so that we are shaken by what happened. Whether the writer intended it or not, the pathos of the story is as absolute as is that later account of the death of Tamar's brother Absalom, with David's memorable lament, "My son, my son!" (II Samuel 18:33). Our sad observation is that David is not reported as having a comparable emotional reaction to his daughter's agony.

Again and again it is obvious that women are legally property, owned in effect by father, brother, or husband. The tenth commandment includes the injunction "You shall not covet your neighbor's wife," because she, as well as the ox and the ass, was the neighbor's property. This "ownership" helps account for the unbelievable offer Lot makes (recorded in Genesis 19:6-8) when the men of Sodom demand that his male visitors be released to them.

How is it, then, that we have a three-dimensional portrait of Sarah, one that depicts her faults but also her princess-like qualities? Why is Deborah such an outstanding heroine blessed with a multitude of capabilities? How does it happen that Miriam governs in a triumvirate along with Moses and Aaron? Why are we given an Abigail who is so obviously superior to her husband in every way? Why is Huldah recognized as a pre-eminent prophet and authority when the newly discovered Book of the Law needs to be authenticated?

Part of the inspiration of the Bible is that the value and the contributions of women surface as often as they do in a day when men were supposed to be everything and women nothing. God must be amused at the way we and our predecessors discriminate so indiscriminately. Do we accept the implications of a verse such as Genesis 1:27, which tells us that the very image of God in which we are created is both male and female?

When we read the beautiful and moving story of the wise woman of Tekoa (II Samuel 14), are we to take seriously the idea that she was a sort of puppet and that Joab put all those words in her mouth, when in fact it must have been at least a mutual conspiracy? Is there not a possibility, or rather a likelihood, that the poetic Miriam is the composer of the longer "Song of Moses" as well as the brief "Song of Miriam"?

How exciting, then, that God's estimate of women breaks through so frequently in the midst of a book written by men in a culture dominated by men. I have been thrilled as I have written these poems, trying to put myself in the place of each of these women — despite the fact that this may seem all but impossible. Again and again their remarkableness has been revealed to me.

Over one hundred poems appear here, though I wrote many more. The reasons for omission are several, but a primary reason has to do with the length of this volume. If I had included all of the poems I have written about these women, this book would be twice as long as it is. If I had made the collection this encyclopedic, it could have been exhaustive — and exhausting — whereas my hope is to convey the fascination, stimulation, and innovation which the Old Testament women offer.

We have tried to choose the best poems — the ones which may most cogently communicate to you the dynamic qualities, the creativity, the cleverness, and the tremendous talents of these women who deserve our attention and our admiration.

THOMAS JOHN CARLISLE

Eve
AND AFTER

1 Honest-to-God People

GOD'S PURPOSE ————————————

I am obsessed to write and tell their story —
these women with their pathos and their glory —
to open up their novel narrative,
discern the inspiration that they give
or their departure from the kinder norm.
From their chill banishment I would make warm
once more their ingenuity and fire,
communicate a passionate desire
to read the original and recognize again
how women are among the best of "men."

REAL PEOPLE

Those women were complicated.
Implicated in life they were more
than illustrations of one golden
strand of behavior or some
random moment of negligence. Job's wife
is remembered for her bitter
remark which was natural
but not necessarily normative.
Eve has unjust notoriety
for apple-picking but no credit
for curiosity and initiative
and creativity. Noah's wife
went along for the ride
and kept track of the weather reports.
Sarah is simply the spouse
of Abraham until we observe
the variety of her reactions
in episodes we customarily
forget or ignore.

The platitudinous
the stereotyped
the hackneyed
are too easily substituted
(in our mental gymnastics)
for the singular and individualistic
the eccentric and idiosyncratic
and other invigorating characteristics
of real people
made in the heterogeneity of God.

LOOK AT ME

Come, look at me again and try to dream
the woman I was in that far long ago.
My hair style and my dress may set me off
as ancient, but I beg of you to know
the actual person I was—the thoughts which I
carried in my heart—no photograph could show
or artist's sketch—the essentials of my self—
the woman alive in this portfolio.

PROVING THE PERTINENCE

Statistically men
(predictably too)
predominate the text
and concordance
of scripture
but the women
manage to infiltrate
at crucial times
and prove their pertinence
to all the sacred story.

DAUGHTERS OF ZION _____

If there had been
no daughters of Zion
there wouldn't have been
any sons either.

UNBENIGN NEGLECT_____

Those print-filled pages
could have contained
more numerous references
to how she lived
and what she thought
and achieved—
the Colonial woman
the Renaissance woman
the Biblical woman—
but mostly men
managed the editing
and the retention
of what they considered
selectively significant—
and missed so much
by unbenign neglect.

2 *In the Beginning*

A MATTER OF FIDELITY

To be faithful to the first
spectacular and inclusive
chronicle of creation,
observe and cherish
that the Poet of the Universe
chose to compose
people with sufficient
similarity and resemblance
and affinity to their Maker
that *male and female*
is definitively descriptive
and the word *image*
metaphorically appropriate.

Genesis 1:27

EVE

REWARDING

After eliciting
Eve from Adam
God was so pleased
with the achievement
it merited
the rest
of the day
off!

SIDEKICKS

God freed Eve
from being completely
part of Adam
choosing to produce
prime partners
for the new enterprise.

CULMINATION

God *labored*
to produce
the woman —
building her
not from dust
but from the
ready rib —
to consummate
creation
and to set
the new world
right.

Genesis 2:22

INVITATION TO OBEDIENCE _____

Eve
like Adam
failed to live
up
to the hopes
of God.

It is too easy
to choose
the fatal fruit
and to refuse
the truer
nourishment
available.

We too
profane
the garden
and are driven
out
to wrestle
with the weeds
and wilderness
of an intransigent
world.

But providentially
like Eve and Adam
we are accompanied
by One
who made us
and who still
wishes us well.

PRIZED EQUALLY_____

Women can rebel
against God
quite as well
as men.
But let it be
her conscience
striving to determine
and not some man's
convenient dictum
arrogating judgment
(or injustice)
to fit his scheme
for making her
subservient
second-class
inferior
or less than a person
prized equally
by God
in new creation.

ORIGINALS_____

I have stayed awake
thinking of women
who barely make
the pages of the Bible
and whose contribution
may well have been far greater
than the masculine scribes
historians and annalists
were willing to let God
inspire them to detail.

Of Adah and Zillah
at least we know their names
and the melodious appellations
and the significant influence
of their four offspring —
Jabal the rancher and cattle-raiser
Jubal who played the lyre and pipe
and spread the gift of music
and Tubal-Cain the prototype
of every village blacksmith
and munitions maker
while Naamah chanced to get
her name recorded but not
her own original talent
as her brother and half-brothers did.

The father Lamech
qualifies as the first poet
with rhythm and excitement
and wild and wondrous words
which sting and burn
and—sorrowfully—create
a hymn of hate
which all of humankind
has yet to unlearn.

Genesis 4:19-24

11

THE ADMIRAL'S WIFE _____

Noah's wife
is taken
for granite
treated like
a cipher
an insignificancy
a minor appendage
to a nautical
and
salvific
extravaganza.

She's only
Ms. Noah.
Her baptized name
is washed away
by history's fickle flood.
If she believed
the story
God told her husband
we are not told.
We know she went along
without the lust for lingering
or penchant for procrastination
shown by Lot's salty wife
in drier circumstances.

Her function
or office
in the shipyard
is never noted
in the ledgers
or the archives.
Perhaps she read
the blueprints
measured the cubits
handled a hammer,

12

saw, plane, chisel,
kept things level
and on an even keel.
Or was she instead
consigned to manage
the commissary
so virile Noah
and their three strong sons
could concentrate
on carpentry?

Was she aware
the ark
she would embark on
was to be
a floating zoo
a circus carrier
a marine menagerie
and this might entail
a chore or two
for her and also
for their daughters-in-law—
the other Waves
enlisted for the voyage?

Her maritime
commission
is not listed
in the ship's log
but she may
have had to say
"Aye, Aye, Sir"
to the Admiral.
Presumably
she was first mate—
though Noah
may not have known
what that implied.
And what
Shem   Ham   and Japheth
called their wives

may not have been
in navigational
vocabulary.

Did these female
seafarers
carry water
for the elephants
and feed
the chimpanzees
post pollen
for the bees
and give the cats
their Friskies
while keeping the ravens
and the carrier doves
out of paws' reach?

What an exciting
sight —
and sound —
and smell —
these women tasted
when their harbor
of refuge
was hoisted in the rain
by rising waters
and they set sail
for no particular port
since no dry docks
were currently available.
They did keep calling
"Ship ahoy!"
to damp mirages.

Evidently
having the women
on board
was not bad luck
or a Jonah curse
by any stretch
of the imagination

or any manner
of means.
The blessed boat
stayed upright
and watertight.

If someone
knocked on wood
and had a hand
in lifting spirits
and making the voyage
on the briny deep
more sufferable
we can guess
her role
but not her name—
no way!

At last
the sun
came back
the waters
sank
slowly
but certainly
and the determined dove
her second time out
retrieved an olive leaf
and then they knew
they were home free
and could rely
on rainbows
in the future.

One of eight—
(how unfruitful
if this octet
had been
all men
or only women
in contrast

to the balance
of the cargo!) —
one of eight
saved by and from
the water
the unnamed wife
and mother
put her foot down
on dry land
at last
and laughed
and shouted Hallelujah
for this most welcome splashdown
this most sweet re-entry
into a world
she had not really wanted
to leave
or lose.

Genesis 6–8

3 *The Matriarchs*

FIRST WOMAN _____

Sarah was the first
to have her picture
painted and her acts
recorded in detail
and her indispens
ability made clear
to the stupendous
program God proposed.

Genesis 11–23

LOOK TO SARAH _____

Abraham was not
so singularly
important
that any old woman
would do
to bear
the child
of promise.
It had to be
Sarah:
Sarah the devastating
ly beautiful
Sarah the skeptical
Sarah the self-sacrificing
Sarah the steadfast
Sister of the faith-filled
Mother of nations:
Sarah!
Sarah!
Sarah!

Isaiah 51:2

"THE GOD OF SEEING" _____

When Sarah's strategy
backfired in proud success
her mistress' harshness
sent Hagar flying
defiantly for parts unknown.
Yet Yahweh met her
by a sudden spring
between Kadesh and Bered
and sent her back
fortified with wild promises
for her expected son
and his descendants.
She called her visitor
"The God of Seeing"
and the welcome well
"Beer-lahai-roi"—
"Have I indeed seen God
and yet survived?"

Back at the ranch
Hagar bore the baby
but as time went by
Sarah enjoyed an unexpected
pregnancy and Isaac
grew old enough to play
with his half-brother.
Again Sarah exploded.
Abraham with tears
dispatched his concubine
with plenty of bread and water
into the wilderness—
and Ishmael whom he loved
went with his mother.

And when the water was gone
Hagar was sure
her child would die
and left him
under a bush
and walked a bowshot off
so that she would not see.
But Ishmael wept
and God responded:
"Lift up the lad
and hold him tight
and look!
A well of water
waits your lips and his.
You can replenish
your supply and live—
you and your son."

The sharp-eyed Deity
manages to get
around when people least
expect attention—
not just to those
who claim monopoly
of God's good graces.

Genesis 16:1-16; 21:8-21

THE TRIAL _____

        Sarah had laughed
with a glad humor at the late delivery
and loved the boy as though she had expected
for years.
        She would have cried seven cries and died
if she had known the nature of the walk
her son and husband took—the two together.

She did not know the burden that they shared—
the wood the boy could carry on his back,
the torch and knife too dangerous for the lad
searing and cutting the obedient heart
of the vulnerable and all but victim father.

She could not hear their silence as they strode
upon that awful third day of ordeal
nor watch the building of the filial altar,
the binding of the cords, the lifted blade,
the look upon her husband's tortured face
the split second when his name rang out
in the sublime caesura of reprieve,
blessing and unbelievable relief.

I wish we knew what Sarah said to them
when they trudged back from those high holy days
with pieces of the sacrificial ram
fruits of devotion and obedience
and told how close they had come to terminating
the hopes and dreams which she and Abraham shared.

Perhaps at last they had come to know the truth:
They did not own their son. And Abraham
did not own Sarah. And Sarah herself
did not own Abraham. God owned them all.

Genesis 22

SUDDEN THOUGHT

While negotiating
for the burial cave
it hit him hard.
He loved her.
They had known
an incredible
life together—
come to think of it.
He wondered
if he had ever
told her.
Would the four hundred
shekels this rascal
Ephron was asking
begin to make up?
Or could he trust that,
being a woman,
she knew
all along?

Genesis 23

LOT'S WIFE LOOKED BACK _____

Lot's wife looked back at her home city, lit
by a strange glow and a grim fungus cloud;
and when Lot called she had no mouth to answer.

How could she know this blast of fire and brimstone
was more than human eyes could watch and bear?
She had been told. But ears decline belief.

How could her husband trust the men who said
to flee from Sodom since a holocaust
would purge its sin in a hot bath of fire?

Their sons-in-law-to-be had thought them crazy,
jesting with such incredible alarms.
Sodom, they said, was sure to last forever.

Lot and his wife and daughters lingered long
while heaven's sirens screamed and no one heard
except the wards of Abraham's brave prayers.

Angels they must have been who took their hands
and started them to safety past the plain
outside the city they had loved too much.

Flee for your life, they said. *Do not look back
and do not stop one moment in the valley
before you reach the little hillside town.*

Lot's wife looked back at her home city, lit
by a strange glow and a grim fungus cloud;
and when Lot called she had no mouth to answer.

And he and his daughters ran obedient
toward the horizon out of fallout range
of the doomed city of disobedience.

Genesis 19:15-26

23

KEPT AND CHERISHED _____

In his old age
without beloved Sarah
Abraham was lonely.
Remembering
or reinterpreting
the admonition made to Adam
that it was not good
to be alone,
he wed Keturah.

She gave him solace
and companionship
and children whom he did not need
and whom eventually he sent away
provisioned to make their fortunes
elsewhere. But Keturah
he kept and cherished.

Genesis 25:1, 4
I Chronicles 1:32, 33

24

THE NIGHT IS DARK:
Jacob's Prayer to Rebekah _____

The night is dark
and I am far
from hope and near
to fear and death.
O my mother,
teach me to sleep
as the sheep do
home in the fold.
Soften this stone
for my pillow.
Send me a dream
and assure me
that I will find
your father's house.

Feed Esau well,
O my mother.
Tranquilize him
lest he bellow
and follow me
and, red-handed,
avenge my guile.
Let me forget
my clever sin
and sleep a while.

My climb was steep,
O my mother.
These rocky steps
would tear a lamb
to pieces. Give
me peace tonight.
Reach out. Extend
the ladder of
your love. And more,
build me a bridge
to father's God.

Genesis 28

NURSE, HELPER, FRIEND_____

Almost invisible
until we learn
her death and burial place
and the concern
and gratitude
which someone felt
this Deborah had earned—
nurse, helper, friend,
with the Oak of Weeping
near God's dwelling
in Bethel
for her final sleeping.

Genesis 24:59; 35:8

LIKE RACHEL

Like Rachel, God cares for the children.
Like God, Rachel cares for the children.
Her children are God's children.
Her grief is God's grief.
God's grief becomes God's grace.

Jeremiah 31:15 (22)

LEAH

IN DISGUISE

Leah had lovely
eyes—not weak
or witless. Only
in contrast with Rachel
could she be judged
on a lesser level
of acumen
or beauty. Stories
tend to accentuate
the predilections
of the historian.
Some heroines
stay Cinderella
in disguise.
Perhaps Jacob
loved Leah
better than he let on.

27

LOST IN THE LORE

Leah gets lost
or at least sidetracked
in the lore of her people
though it was not Rachel alone
but Rachel and Leah together
along with Bilhah and Zilpah
who built up the house of Israel.
Never underestimate
the stamina of the tender
mother of seven
whose line has gone out
through all the earth.

OUR SISTER DINAH

If Dinah
were our sister
would we care
what Dinah wanted
or must she
be treated
as a piece
of property—
a pawn
and not
a person?

Genesis 34

GOD WAS NOT SHOCKED
(Genealogical Observation) _____

We wonder
whether Tamar
was justified
in making
her father-in-law
produce the fruit
his promises enjoined.

But Judah came
to the contrite conclusion
that she
contrived to be
considerably more righteous
than he had been.

And later generations
rejoiced remembering
her wit
her ingenuity
and her success
and gave one twin
honorable mention
in the story of Ruth
as well as headlines
in the house
and lineage
of David.

Genesis 38

29

4 Egypt, Exodus, and Entry _____

THE PLIGHT OF POTIPHAR'S WIFE ___

Oh, Joseph, you and I might well have been
lovers whose epic Egypt would remember
past pyramids and pharaohs but you chose
your God's embrace as preferable to mine.
Now while you languish in the palace prison
I languish here tormented by the tantrum
that led me to betray you. And still I burn
to share the uttermost planets of your dreams.

Genesis 39

ASENATH

EGYPTIAN BRIDE_____

Oh, Joseph, I am of so little use to you
except to attend you on such state occasions
wives are required. Yes I have borne two sons
more expeditiously than your dear mother did.
Ephraim and Manasseh promise your permanence
at least one generation longer while your dreams
say they will persist through history. Perhaps.
I'm glad you came to Egypt but I wish
I rated better than fifth in your esteem.
Your self, your God, and Pharaoh—and your job—
take precedence and priority over me.

Genesis 41:45; 46:20

THE WIT AND WISDOM OF
THE MIDWIVES_____

The story of exodus and liberation
starts with the rather civil disobedience
of two heroic women, valiant midwives—
Shiphrah and Puah.

With subtle strategy they tantalized,
enraged, outflanked, outwitted
the macho ruler, Hitler of ancient Egypt,
who sought to liquidate an entire people.
They broke his cruel decree while blithely claiming
innocence and ignorance and impotence
regarding salvage of the newborn males
of Hebrew parentage.

"It is the mothers' fault, not ours," they protested
when he accused them of malfeasance.
"It is the mothers' crime, so strong they are,
so able to deliver themselves
they bear their boys before we reach their birthstools.
And then they smuggle off these latest progeny
without permission or consent from us."

The mighty monarch could not manage
an answer to their artifice.
Heroic Shiphrah and heroic Puah—
and even more heroic if they were
Egyptian instead of Hebrew—
mutually supportive in their conscientious
objection to the king's command to kill
while their vocation was to bring to birth,
to abet God's purpose in the whole creation.

Almost anonymous, too long ignored,
the powerless who used the power they had—
we hail them as the staunch inaugurators
and initiators—the founding fore- and foster-
mothers of exodus and liberation
so many years before the floating infant
was finally prepared for holy orders
and took the tremendous liberty
of enabling his persecuted people
to steal away.

Exodus 1:15-22

MOSES' ADOPTIVE MOTHER

PHARAOH'S DAUGHTER_____

Did Pharaoh's daughter
live to see the son
she salvaged from the river
challenge his grandfather
(or some successor)
with ten grisly plagues
and lead his independence
party through the Sea
of Reeds off to a land
of sand and hidden oil
where postal service
would never reach him
with the lonely letters
of urgent mother love
solicitude for safety
and fervor for his future?

She may have suffered
a traumatic shock
when her superior son—
her adoptee—
did not turn out to be
a second Joseph
for old Egypt's empire.
Instead, refusing to strangle
ethnic identity
he proceeded
to murder
a native bully
and became
a fugitive
from the injustice
of a land of bondage.

However long she lived
she never would know
just what the cute moist infant
she cuddled in her arms
down by the sacred river
would at last
amount to.

Exodus 2

ACCREDITATION _____

Miriam's brief biography
(in Exodus and Numbers)
gives her minimal mention
considering—
or not considering—
her contributions
and her character.

We encounter hints
and intimations
of her finesse
and her sagacity
and versatility,
her skill in music
and her power in poetry
as well as her esteemed position
in the hearts
of all her people.

She was a chief
executive—
one of three—
as we discover
when we read
between the lines.

Why should we need
to toil so arduously
in order to surmise
and recognize
her stature?

MIRIAM
(In Fifty Words or Less)

Supportive sister
who guided the pitch-patched ark
to the King's daughter

Emancipation's
mouthpiece singing victory
in words she fashioned

Government sharer
skillful administrator
in triumvirate

Moses' challenger—
in company with Aaron—
no march without her

Blend of tenderness
and toughness this Miriam
poet and prophet.

Exodus 2, 15; Numbers 12; 20:1; 26:59; Micah 6:4

ZIPPORAH
DESERT BRIDE

Moses was a hero
but not much of a husband,
an illustrious lawgiver
but an indifferent lover.

Or else the fault
may have been Zipporah's
in a no-fault situation.

Maybe any woman would have been
a mismatch with a driven man who had
such mountainous matters on his mind!

Exodus 2:15-22; 4:25; 18:1-12

BLUE, PURPLE, AND SCARLET _____

The wise-hearted women used their creativity
to beautify the tabernacle,
the tent of meeting, the holy place of God—
the blue, the purple, and the scarlet.
Color and texture—all to God's glory.

They brought their brooches and their earrings,
resplendent pendants, ornaments of gold.
No offering too good for Yahweh's House.
But best of all (even as with the men)
the giving of their hands *and* of their hearts.

Each used her special skill
whatever it might be—
and this is still our scarlet
blue and purple opportunity.

Exodus 35:20-29
(Note that the women are not mentioned
in the parallel passage in Exodus 25:1-9.)

THE GRACE OF SERVING_____

The women ministered—we are not told
the details of their service but we bless
one chronicler who happened to remember
this instance of their zeal and willingness.

In the image of our Creator, male and female,
all colors, all races, all people are embraced.
How can the God of all receive our gifts
when we exclude one giver as ungraced?

Exodus 38:8
(Note that the women are not mentioned
in the parallel passage in Exodus 30:18ff.)

37

LAST LAUGH _____

What's funny in Leviticus? Not much
unless you chuckle at the closing chapter
where a woman's worth is figured at three-fifths
of a man's. Oddly, eccentrically,
but equally we match inequity.
Who's laughing then or now? Who has the right?

Leviticus 27:1-8

MAHLAH, NOAH, HOGLAH, MILCAH, AND TIRZAH

THE DAUGHTERS OF ZELOPHEHAD___

The daughters of Zelophehad came running up to Moses.
"Your law is fabulous," they said, "but our research discloses
that for the women of our land it's still no bed of roses.

"How come that when a father dies, his sons by right inherit
but if he has no sons, no matter how his daughters merit,
the property reverts to men? Are we not fit to share it?"

Wise Moses scratched his head. "You're right as rain
    or snow or thunder.
How I could overlook the rights of folks like you, I wonder.
It's not too late to rectify my unintended blunder.

"Daughters henceforth will rate as well—providing
    they've no brothers.
Go, Mahlah, Noah, Hoglah, Milcah, Tirzah, you be mothers.
Your father's property shall stay with you, not pass
    to others."

38

The men who would have profited were clever politicians:
"Suppose these women marry men from other tribes.
　　　Conditions
should be attached to counteract land transfers and
　　　partitions."

"These women may marry whom they like," ruled Moses,
　　　"choose their man
except that he must chance to be a member of their clan
and not some son of Issachar or Benjamin or Dan."

And so they won their point apart from that
　　　severe restriction
which seemed to them unjust and cruel and quite
　　　a contradiction
and goes to show that women's rights can be less
　　　fact than fiction.

Numbers 27:1-11; 36:1-12

RAHAB

FAITH *AND* WORKS _____

Rahab's faith and works combine and conspire
to make her one of the progenitors
of those who trust God's vision and at risk
obey the daily assignments which contribute
to the reign of God beyond our present seeing
but not beyond the reach of our believing.

Joshua 2:1-24; 6:17, 22-25
Matthew 1:5; Hebrews 11:31; James 2:25

5 *In the Days of the Judges*_____

A TALE OF THREE WOMEN _____

Sisera's mother
stands watch at the window
arranges the blinds
to see clearly his coming
dust in the distance
from one thousand chariots
and one thousand charioteers.
Then she envisions
her son as a conqueror
riding before them
and bringing the booty—
a maiden or two
for each one of his soldiers
and all sorts of dyed stuffs
embroidery, needlework.
Some of the best
he will give to his mother.

Sisera's mother
peers through the lattice.
"Why is it later
than my son predicted?
Why aren't the war horses
on the horizon?
Why are their hoofbeats
not heard in the distance?
Quiet is ominous.
What can delay him?"

Her ladies-in-waiting
keep trying to tell her
what she has been trying
to tell to herself:
"His army is busy.
Yes, Sisera is busy
in finding and binding
deciding, dividing

and loading the loot
on available carts.
Such labor takes longer."
But why does he tarry?

Sisera's mother
is waiting
is waiting
certain of conquest
but waiting uneasily
although their weak foes
are so poorly prepared
ineffectively armed
for the unequal contest—
no chariots, no horses
no weapons of valor
the tribes of the Hebrews
inept, disunited.
These faint-hearted scullions
would not battle now
were it not for a woman
a judge of the people
the prophetess Deborah
(What knows she of battle?)
with faint-hearted Barak
her gritless commander
reluctant to venture
unless she goes with him
to shore up the struggle.
"But why does he tarry
my son the brave general?"

Sisera's mother
believes in the bloodshed:
"Whoever contends
with my son and his chariots
can count themselves lucky
to sneak off alive
away from their comrades
who cannot survive
the bruises

the wounds
and the havoc
of battle.
My son will not suffer
a cut or a scratch.
He will come home in triumph.
But why does he tarry
and leave me so utterly
tense, apprehensive?"

Sisera's mother
is watching and waiting.
Uninformed
unsuspecting
his mother knows nothing.
No intelligence trickles
back from the battle.
His mother knows nothing
of stars in their courses
the legions of heaven
who fight for the ragtag
who challenge his army.
His mother knows nothing
of streams overflowing
and wild watercourses
eroding terrain
where the wheels of the chariots
are muddied and mired.
The horses sink down
in the slosh and the ooze
and the slime of the cloudburst.

Sisera's mother
is waiting and watching
from high palace windows—
no glimmer
no inkling
and no premonition
no mystic clairvoyance
to divine
and distinguish

her son
as he flounders
through hailstones
and muck
to take flight
from the forces
he thought
would be victim
and vanquished
long before now.
She cannot observe him
deserting his tropps
alone, unattended
to find higher ground
and refuge at last
in the tent of a Kenite
(presumably friendly
to Sisera's people)
in the tent of one Jael
whose husband was Heber.
Despite his sad plight
how relieved she would be
at this fortunate rescue.

Sisera's mother
would have sighed
with elation
if she could have witnessed
the cool hospitality
Jael provided.
When Sisera asked
only water
she opened
a generous milkskin
and fed him
with curds
in a lordly bowl.
She bade him relax
from his ache
and exhaustion.

"Stand at the door
of the tent,"
he instructed,
"and say there is no one
around but yourself
if pursuers are questioning.
So let me sleep
and recover
my strength
for I am half-dead."

Sisera's mother
would have cried
seven cries
and expired
in heartstroke
if she had been privy
to the subsequent
service of Jael
who picked up
a sharp tent peg
and hoisted a hammer
and serenely accosted
the sleeping commander
and pounded unmercifully
the peg through his temple
and into the earth
then casually strolled
from the tent
and met Barak
(whom Deborah
had emboldened
and inspired
and bolstered
and buttressed).
She invited him in
to the tent
to encounter
face to face
the dead son
of Sisera's mother.

Sisera's mother!
Who brought her the message
her son was all done
with his life of destruction?
Did anyone
sing her
the song
of seer Deborah
who ascribed to her God
all the power
and the glory
and the means
to deliver
her people
from evil,
the duress
and atrocities
of their oppressors?
Sleep and rest,
bereaved mother.
Sleep and rest.

Awake, awake
O Deborah
bee of the Lord
who trusted
God's might
and God's purpose
you who awoke
God's people
to burst
from their bondage
you who prevailed
upon Barak
(the latent lightning)
and induced him
to march
with ten thousand
from the tormented tribes
of the children of Israel

and swoop down
like thunder
from lofty Mount Tabor.

Awake, awake
O Deborah.
Strike up the band.
Burst into song.
March on
O my soul
with strength.
Now is the time
for a hymn
of thanksgiving.
Glorify God
with cymbals and singing
God the Creator
of heaven and earth
God who directs
the full clouds
to drop water
the mountains
to quake
and the world
to tremble
and women and men
to obey.
March on
O my soul
with strength.

O God
may all of your enemies
perish
like the fanatic forces
of Sisera.
Let your friends
all be as the sun
in his glorious rising.

Judges 4-5

47

JAEL

Jael
with her curds
and whey
and hammer
and tent peg
makes a motherly
model
(when she's
on our side)
for chivalrous
demolition
experts.

THE MILLSTONE CONNECTION:
Sic Semper Tyrannis _____

Abimelech's bloody career
was brought to a grinding halt
by a stout-hearted
and heavy-handed woman
who cast her vote
against his reign
of terrorism
by hefting her household's
upper millstone
to Thebez' rampart tower
where she took dead aim
and dropped it down
upon the royal skull.

She was the judge
passing the capital sentence
which carried so much weight.

He was embarrassed
to be so grievously wounded
by a mere woman
so he asked
his armor-bearer
to dispatch him.
He might better
have been mortified
by his own maniac
behavior.

The millstone grounded him!

Judges 9:50-56
II Samuel 11:21

HIS ONLY CHILD _____

"She was his only child" and yet his vow
meant more to him. He would have said his faith,
his faith in God—in God!—required her death.
We look with anger on the story now
and call it folly. There must have been a way
to avoid the vow or void the vow when he
returned to celebrate his victory.
Dancing she came. Why did he have to say
that *she* had caused the trouble by her joy
and eagerness and love? What unconcern
for how she felt! And why should she in turn
accept the doom? If she had been a boy
would he have survived the father's fatal word?
But she had the bad luck to be a daughter.
So slaughter is followed by senseless slaughter.
We are no better at seeing the absurd
and crude and cruel in our current state.
We make them die and then we praise their dying
and think we pay them by that glorifying.
Can we retract our vows before it is too late?

Judges 11

MANOAH'S WIFE AND THE DIVINE VISITOR

To see
was not to fear—
and God's arrival
was no intrusion
or intimidation.
Greeting was grace
and presence, providence.
She felt wholly at home
with the divine
visitor.
She paid
all heed to God
and God paid heed
to her.
Seeing
was not a threat
but a reward.

Judges 13

THE FIVE WOMEN
IN SAMSON'S LIFE _____

All of the women
in Samson's story—
his God-visited mother,
his transient wife,
his wife's sad sister,
the harlot of Gaza,
the wily Delilah—
were simply adjuncts
to his comical adventures
and foils to his follies.

He didn't know how
to treat a lady
or carry off
a decent relationship.

What a man!

Judges 13-16

THE LEVITE'S CONCUBINE

HINTS OF HOLOCAUST_____

The partitioning of the Levite's concubine
and what preceded all that cruel night
do not belong to humane history
but they are there and strive to startle and shame us
with the dark depths we casually ignore
lest we observe our liability
for tolerating liquidation or incineration
of any of God's persecuted children.

Judges 19

6 *The Romance of Ruth:* Poems about Naomi, Orpah, and Ruth _____

THE WAY I WAS_____

You who seemed my enemy
when your drought and famine forced me
to live in the presence of my enemies.
You whose decrees of death
one by one removed my dearest
till none was left near to cherish
or comfort or care for my soul—
or so it seemed.

My God, You were still my friend
and yet I could not see it
even in the Ruth whom You gave me
who responded with your kind of giving,
even in the joy of the journey
that took me back to my homeland
and the well and the fields of my fathers
and mothers whose heritage
of faith was part of your blessing.

My God, You were still my friend
even when I could not fathom
the course You would take to restore me.
I misprized the jewel of hope
but You crowned me with kindness and honor.

And I praise You
for not giving up
on me
when I
gave up on You.

HURLER OF ACCUSATIONS _____

Like Job
Naomi hurled
her accusations
at the mountain God
whose clenched demands
and jealous judgments
had turned her youthful joy
to bitterest sorrow.
It was God's
prerogative
to judge and damn—
though in a brighter day
to judge and bless—
and hers to remonstrate
with all the fever
of her fragile faith.
"You had too much
to do with me
when I
took little thought
of You and your
requirements.
It isn't fair
to single me out,
my agonizing and divine
Antagonist
El Shaddai.
Is it too late
to set aside
or supersede
your verdict?"

OUT OF THE DEPTHS

Out of the depths
I cried
and told You, God,
that nothing
absolutely nothing
could be done
to get me out
and up.
The chilly facts
confirmed
my scuttled hope.
I was awash
with all your waves
and billows
your absurd
irrational
unreasonable
buffetings.
What worse could happen
than what already
had laid me low?
And why should I
look for the bright side
when all sides were dark
and all I had
in all the world
was You?

DON'T BURDEN ME
(Naomi to her Daughters-in-law)_____

Seeing to myself
is all
and then some.
Go back
and cry alone
and let me try
to dry my own
and find a pittance
that I need
not share.
Entreat me not
to carry
your burden too.
My prayer
is fully
occupied
with my dilemma
and with my distress.
There is not room
for you
within
my wilderness.

HOW EASILY A LOVE ABORTS_____

Let me be Orpah if I cannot be
Ruth or Naomi or some treasured name
in annals of romance or history.
Not everyone can be the heroic same.
Even though I walk back to my mother's house
seconding Chilion's mother that this course
is wiser if I hope to find a spouse,
I would not live resentment and remorse
far from my friends and my accustomed place
simply to prove a loyalty of sorts.
I could not stand the taunts of alien race.
I love Naomi and she means me well
and knows how easily a love aborts
when driven to deeds beyond the feasible.

Ruth 1:4-15

NOT NEVER

Never again,
said Naomi
in her hungry heart,
Never again
a man to know
or sons to honor.

Never ever
a grandchild
or a home
with three
or even two
dimensions.

Never again
enough
of food
security
insured
and certain.

The barren land
the barren home
the barren womb—
How can I bear
the doubtful blessing
of longevity?

So right
and yet
so wrong.
A daughter-in-law
might love and be
better than seven sons.

NOT FORTY YEARS _____

Not forty years across the wilderness
nor even forty days, Naomi, Ruth
traveling alone, childless and husbandless,
near the Dead Sea of canceled love and youth.
A week, a fortnight at the very most
brought hastening Jordan to refreshing sight,
blest, they believed, by the bright heavenly host.
The Bethlehemite crossed with the Moabite
and journeying farther found that little town
where shepherds watch their flocks and fields increase
with wheat and barley, gleaning they can own
and know the promises of hope and peace.
And this is all they ask when first they come
begging of the House of Bread a widow's crumb.

YOU, RUTH _____

You, Ruth, who knew you could not stand to stay
a stranger in your land whose gods seemed strange
once Mahlon praised the God of Abraham,
the God of promise and the God of change
who followed the people—rather, went before
filling their sky with challenges, commands,
and comforts; whom no idol could depict;
who lived among them in whatever lands
they were led to or through. This God who gave
Naomi strength to leave her husband's grave
and both her sons' last resting-place assured
that she would find wherever she might go
the power and presence of Creation's Lord
even in the midst of bitterness and woe.
I too discover my little gods too small,
I too a pilgrim, stranger and bereft
set out for new horizons and some strange
belittled Bethlehem. Will I be left
lorn in my going out, my coming in?
Or am I given to glean my grains of truth,
encounter compassion in some foreign face,
by God's grace gain an inheritance as did Ruth?

YOU WERE A STRANGER_____

Whether from justice or from kindness let
the needy, stranger, widow, fatherless
glean in your fields. Their table must be set
lest you in your own luxury forget
you were a stranger, you were in distress.

PLEASANT TO YOUR TASTE _____

I bring you bread, dear Boaz.
I ground the flour fine
from the grain I gleaned, dear Boaz,
in your fields in the bright sunshine.
You gave me the grain for the gleaning
here in the House of Bread.
Smell the fragrance of this loaf
and eat, dear Boaz, be fed
by the bread we prepared together
you and the Lord and I.
And entreat me not to leave you.
Let me live where you live and die
in the land you love and that loves you
as proved by this harvesting.
And let me be pleasant to your taste
as well as the bread I bring.

NOT LIKE DELILAH _____

Not like Delilah ready to ensnare
her hero lover for the Philistines—
"So what if I should lay his secret bare;
my patriot purpose justifies my means."
Ruth wrestled with her conscience lest she use
her loveliness like some cheap bag of tricks.
It struck her as a startling piece of news
how love and politics might fairly mix.
That Boaz wise as in some ways he was
should fail to recognize the chance in store
led her, obedient to Naomi's cause,
to throw herself down on his harvest floor.
When he awakes there suddenly occurs
the best solution to his need and hers.

PROPOSAL _____

Was there a harvest moon that noisy night
when Ruth went seeking out where Boaz lay,
wondering if what she did was really right
but certain in her heart she knew the way
and confident that he should recognize
the love he had been feeling all along
but failed to visualize or vocalize.
She hummed a happy love and harvest song
but hushed when by the open threshing floor
she found her benefactor deep in dreams.
Visitor, conspirator, solicitor
of the free grace that rescues and redeems.
His *Who are you?* is followed by the smile
which proves that he has loved her all the while.

RISE UP, MY LOVE, MY FAIR ONE
(Boaz' Song to Ruth) _____

Rise up, my love, my fair one. Come away.
The winter of my witlessness is past.
My concentration on the harvest may
have made me heedless but I see at last.
The mist that filmed my mind is over, gone.
The fairest of flowers appears and it is you.
The singing in my heart has me undone
and I am glad and now know what to do.
The figs have ripened. Vines are in full bloom.
Their fruit and fragrance are as naught to all
your luxury which floods away my gloom
and makes me more than eager for your call.
Arise, my love, my fair one. Come away.
This day of days shall be our wedding day.

RUTH'S WEDDING SONG _____

Now once upon a time within that land
flowing with milk and honey by repute,
a woman came and tried her alien hand
gleaning grain left for poor and destitute.
Widowed she was and beautiful and young
and a sad stranger far away from home.
"Honey and milk are underneath your tongue.
Your lips, my bride, are as the honeycomb"
were words she did not know or hear at first,
for all was strange and few would welcome her
and most were ready to believe the worst.
Her coming brought a murmur and a stir.
From well to field her strangenesses were flung.
And some, in spite, said, "Foreigner, go home."
"Honey and milk are underneath your tongue.
Your lips, my bride, are as the honeycomb"
were words reserved for others. Faithful still
she gleaned and shared her harvest day by day
with her loved mother-in-law who bent her skill
to contrive the redeeming of her protégée.
So came an hour when Ruth herself heard sung
by Boaz as he brought her to their home,
"Honey and milk are underneath your tongue.
Your lips, *my bride,* are as the honeycomb."

(Song of Solomon 4:11)

GREAT-GRANDMOTHER_____

She taught her great-grandchild to make a sling
and how to say the fairest words and sing
them in a world of struggle and despair.
She taught him how to persevere and care
and never guessed he'd grow to be a king.

7 The Beginnings of Monarchy

HANNAH'S MORNING PRAYERS_____

"I am *not* drunk," she said.
"I pray as best I can
to the God you represent
as listening to patient
and persistent prayers.
I thought that God
might hear my pain
and my petition
but to you
my passionate lips
seemed fuddled and tipsy
and no wonder
so confused, beset, I am
by my bleak curse
of childlessness.
I promise God
to give my son
if God will only
give a son to me."

Eli, himself beset
by a different category
of family problem—
sons he could not handle—
offered her his blessing,
sent her on her way
convinced that he would never hear
of her again.

I Samuel 1

MISCONCEPTION _____

There is an unkind
kind of exultation—
the heartless gloating
which Peninnah
exhibited because—
by chance or providence—
she could conceive
easily and often.

I Samuel 1:4-8

THE MOTHER OF ICHABOD _____

God's glory does not vanish
when a sacred ark is stolen or captured
or the best book burned by the blasphemous
or when hope is maimed and dignity defaced
even by the greedy and degenerate.

The wife of Phinehas could not face the fact
when defeat encompassed her on every side.
The ark was conquered and her father-in-law
had died at the shock of it.
The husband who had failed her was dead too—
an inept and unfit guardian of the ark.

Her pain was not the excruciating labor
which she must undergo. Her pain was in
the horror of her utter hopelessness.
She thought that God had gone
because the ark was gone.
She could not comprehend that God cannot
be banished or vanquished or otherwise
terminated or concluded.
She did not have the strength
to see that this was true
and life had bludgeoned her too long and often
for her to find a further reason for living,
and so she named her newborn son
Ichabod—meaning *the glory has departed.*
She died with desperation on her lips
because she had deduced God's glory was gone
because she thought that God was dead
at least for her—perhaps for Israel.

I Samuel 4

NOT QUITE

The young man
with the harp
and shepherd songs
sang to her father
and enamored Michal.

But she was impotent
in her infatuation
until her sister Merab's marriage
meant she could be the prize
to further Saul's ambitions.

If only this love story
might have ended there
we could assume they lived
most happily ever after.
Life isn't quite like that!

I Samuel 18:17-25; 19:11-17; 25:44
II Samuel 3:13-16; 6:12-23

AND STILL I WONDER

And still I wonder
if his bringing me back
was just a power play
to reinforce
his right to the throne
since I was daughter of Saul—
or was there still
a spark of that deep love
he felt for me
and I for him back when
we both were young
and our experience
was meager but so full
of romance and of hope.

II Samuel 6:12-23

69

DEAR ABBY _____

Some men
are so proficient
at being a man
by some perverse
misguided definition
that they break the hearts
of women who have more
intrinsic warmth
and clear perception
of what it really means
to be a person.

And such was Abigail
the wife of Nabal
who tried to save her husband
from his crude and stupid ego.
He waxed so angry
at her timely intervention
that he committed suicide
by apoplexy
and left her free
to love a David
who appreciated
her keen and clever mind
almost as much
as her bewitching beauty.

I Samuel 25:1-42

LISTEN TO ME _____

"I have listened to you,"
said the medium of Endor
to famished and frightened Saul.
"Now you listen to me.
Even if this turns out to be
your last supper,
eat and be thankful.
I am killing a fatted calf
and I am baking
fresh and fragrant bread.
Not only are you a king
who has suffered much—
for all your mistakes
you united your nation
in an era of anarchy—
but you are also a person
and you are hungry
and dead tired.
Listen to me.
Do not refuse
my gift of hospitality
and hope."

I Samuel 28:7-25

METAMORPHOSIS_____

There is a decided
difference between
the young Bathsheba
guilelessly going
to be undone
and the experienced
and wily woman
who badgered the King
to give the throne
to her beloved son
Prince Solomon.

II Samuel 11:1-27; 12:24
I Kings 1:11-40

JONADAB REGARDING TAMAR_____

My name is Jonadab. I have
a sinking feeling I am not
as clever as I like to think.
I encouraged Amnon, my good friend,
to do the most foolish thing
that he was capable of doing—
trying to make him happy.
And now no one is happy
given the way my royal cousin
followed my arrogant advice—
assaulted his half-sister Tamar
in his secret suite and found it
not as sweet or satisfying
as he had dreamed, and spurned her
unheroically. I know
I do not know just how she feels
except that she is stricken
as a doe that will recover
not now or any tomorrow.

Amnon is sicklier and sadder
than he was before he took her
and he will die not from disease
but from the deed to which I spurred him.
Poor Amnon. Poorer Tamar.
And I am poorer and impurer
than any man has a good right
to be.

II Samuel 13:1-22

THE WISE WOMAN OF TEKOA
OFFERS A PEACE PROPOSAL
TO KING DAVID _____

Why let the vicious circle still revolve—
eye for an eye, tooth for a tooth, and death
for a death? Revenge without resolving
the interminable and fatal quarrel.

We will all die. We are like water spilled
upon the ground, which cannot be reclaimed.
Listen to a mother. Listen, O my king.
You who would spare my son for God's sake
spare yours and make this a peaceable kingdom.

II Samuel 14

GOD'S PARABLES _____

We must all die.
We are like water spilt
upon the ground.
We cannot be
recovered
and reclaimed.
But can we be
redeemed?

Our guilt
is not
that we are mortal
but that we die
to love
and intimacy
with God
and even
our dearest own.

We banish ourselves
when we evict
one God-child
from the circle
of our care.

Our God devises
strategies
to circumvent
the twist
of our estrangements.

II Samuel 14:14

74

PERCIPIENT PEACEMAKER_____

The United Nations
could utilize the courage
and diplomatic talents
and mediative methods
of the Wise Woman of Abel.

II Samuel 20:1-2, 14-22

THE STEADFAST LOVE OF RIZPAH_____

Rizpah, whose name means glowing coal
or heated stone or family bread
baked in the ashes—and whose sole
loyalty was to Saul and, with Saul dead,
to Abner briefly—saw her two sons die
when David tried to expiate
Saul's unrecorded treachery
against the Gibeonites. Their hanging fate
tore at her heart and so by day and night
she guarded the corpses from the birds of prey
and beasts—the vulture and the kite,
the jackal and the crow which came that way.
From April harvest till the rain
that falls in autumn Rizpah does her best
but when only the bones remain,
David orders them put to rest
with those of Saul and Jonathan.
Indomitable Rizpah has done all she can.

II Samuel 21:1-14

DAVID TO ABISHAG _____

Will you warm an old man
give him courage and sense
to keep the trembling fires
from vanishing utterly?
I dream of hills and harps
of sheep and scepters
of giants and rogues and comrades
and sons and wives and battles.
My memories meld.
I sleep and waken
sleep and waken
until I cannot tell
which thoughts are earth
and which are air.
Can there be fire again
in this old brain
and rotting body?
Abishag. Is that your name?
Are you the hearth for my chill frame?
Can you re-light the flame
to bring me back
to manhood and desire?

I Kings 1:1-4, 15

ABISHAG TO DAVID _____

I am afraid, my lord. I am afraid.
How can I keep you warm when nothing else
can circulate your blood? Your doctors chose me
and I am flattered by their generous words
about my beauty though I blush to hear them.
But I believe it is rather for my skill—
at least my competence—for being nurse
that I am selected for this royal service.
"What did you say?" you ask. "What did you say?"
Just never mind. It doesn't really matter.
My name is Abishag and I have come
from a far village in your kingdom. Now
go back to bed and I will lie beside you
and let you dream that summer has returned
and those glad days when vigor filled your veins
and none could match your ardor or your power.
I will protect you from the visitors
who wear you down with gossip and demands.
I'll make hot broth when you are ready for it
and sing a lullaby of Bethlehem
and plump your pillow. No, I don't. I don't
know how to play a harp but I can sing
and will right now so you may fall asleep.
And when you do I shall forget my fear
forget my youth, forget my ache for home.
"Home, did you say?" Yes, Home. You said yourself
you would be dwelling in God's house—
     God's home—forever.

I Kings 1:1-4, 15

MOTHER AND CHILD_____

Solomon grinned
at his own grim wisdom
when he ordered
an even split
of the disputed
personal property.

Half is never enough
where human life
is concerned.

The genuine mother
acknowledged that
when she yelled out
that she would yield
her son to save him.

Love doesn't do things
by halves.

I Kings 3:16-28

THE OTHER MOTHER _____

The other mother
was a lover too
not only of strange men
but of the unwanted baby.

The trauma of his death
inspired her deceit.
His smothered corpse
awoke her warmth.

With sudden passion
she wanted a child
in the worst way
to nestle and need her —

78

so uncontrollably
she stole the infant
who was not hers.

Befuddled by grief
she lied for love.

I Kings 3:16-28

THE QUEEN OF SHEBA ⸺⸺⸺⸺⸺

Her dark beauty
her scintillating conversation
her range of riddles
and kaleidoscopic questions,
her diplomatic acumen
her pleasant poise
plus all her wealth
of courtiers and camels
of gold and jewels
and expensive spices
combined to captivate
and to convince King Solomon
in all his storied glory
that he had met a monarch
after his own heart.

She hung on his words
as assiduously as he on hers.

She was more than eager
to see his kingdom
and his coin collection
and sample his wisdom.

He treasured her visit
long after she departed—
and so do we.

I Kings 10:1-13

8 Praise, Love, and Wisdom:
An Interlude_____

GOD'S HANDMAIDEN _____

My mother was God's handmaiden.
She made it her business
to love God
all ways.

Service was her specialty
and Jesus her inspiration
for befriending people
and sharing love and caring
as if it were a matter of course.

Her home was God's house
and God's house was her home
and she was hopeful
she would dwell there always.

The Psalmist has nothing on me.
I too am the child of God's handmaid.

Psalm 116:16 (86:16)

MY MOTHER'S JEWELRY BOX _____

I am looking for my mother's jewelry box—
casket they would have called it once—not cask
(see barrel) nor casque (see helmet) but something
    with locks
and a plush interior among whose contents I ask
Why this? Why that? Why did you choose such trinkets
which nothing can rhyme with distinctly, nothing can save—
these rings, this pendant, this watch that will not
      bear watching?
Ordinarily I associate a casket with a grave.
But this says something of you—a woman—my mother—
stones that are living and colors which warm and shine
when light is upon them and flesh. One after another
I draw them up from your precious and private mine.
I would think I would want to leave them all together
but you would desire them scattered among the young—
your granddaughters, wives of your grandsons, but not
    this evening.
The love of you is in my heart and on my tongue
with no one to tell except myself and—if you are listening—
you who planted them here through the jeweled years—
amethyst, chrysoprase, and diamonds glistening
and sapphires and rubies, and pearls which encase my tears.

LIKE A FRUITFUL VINE _____

The God-fearing man
according to the Psalmist
shall have a loving wife
who like a fruitful vine
growing within the very heart
of his abode shall bless him
with her presence.
Admirable
and wonderful if
concurrently
she has good reason
to thank God for him.

Psalm 128:3

PRETTY PICTURE_____

If a beautiful woman
without discretion
is like a gold ring
in a pig's snout,
how shall we characterize
the handsome but insensitive
and witless man?

Proverbs 11:22

SONG OF SONGS_____

O my beloved, there is none like you,
locked in the holy of holies of my heart.
You are as wondrous as the morning dew
new every morning. May each morning start
for me with your assistance and your grace.
You the unattainable in my dream
but breathing now beside me face to face.
How did you ever, my beloved, deem
me worthy to share your mountains and your deep
valleys, your pastures and your living food?
Even when in weariness I fall asleep
my heart is waking. Every passing mood,
every emotion alchemized by your
warm presence when I come and realize
you are the joy I have been longing for.
I find my self when I look in your eyes
or touch your hand or feel your glowing cheek.
You are the meaning that I understand.
You are the eager words my soul would speak.
And there is none as fair in all the land.
Your banquet house my sweetest destination.
Here let me come and stay forever, feed.
You the pleasant fruit of all my fascination.
Your banner over me is all I need.

Song of Solomon

EVERY TIME AND EVERY WHERE _____

For you are fair, my love. Yes, you are fair
and all the years add only to your grace.
My love is every time and every where.

You are the remedy to my despair.
Night disappears when I can see your face
for you are fair, my love. Yes, you are fair.

Of time's tall sum I would not be aware
since days with you provide their own sweet pace.
My love is every time and every where.

You were the answer to my childhood prayer.
That joy no circumstances can erase
for you are fair, my love. Yes, you are fair.

You taught me how to love and how to care.
Because you give me scope and grant me space
my love is every time and every where.

And so today again I would declare
my ecstasy in your renewed embrace
for you are fair, my love. Yes, you are fair.
My love for you is every time and every where.

9 *North and South*

HELPED BY THE HELPLESS _____

She didn't need
to share his faith
or nationality
to be a source
of fortitude
and food.

Why are we
so particular
when our best
resource may be
the outcast
or the stranger?

Good God
help us to be
helped by the helpless
nurtured by those
whose "nothing"
multiplies
and succors
our starved souls
and sets us back
upon our forward journey.

I Kings 17:8-24
Luke 4:26

THE PROPHET'S WIDOW DISCOVERS
THE OIL OF GLADNESS _____

I who had borrowed too much
was asked to borrow
as many empty vessels
as could be found
among my friends and neighbors
and fill them
with the little oil I had—
and God would do the rest.
Impossible!

How can it be?
The oil pours on and on
like a rich gusher
in a new-tapped well.
Every last jar is filled
before the free-flow ceases
and I can sell the oil
to pay my debts
and save my beloved sons
from slavery.

Elisha's God—and mine—
can multiply resources,
banish sorrow,
bring happiness and hope,
unshackle our compassion
so we fill
the empty cups of others
who will find blessing
through the wonder
and miracle
of our sharing.

II Kings 4:1-7

COLLABORATOR

God employs
the little slave girl
who believes the love
and latitude of God
and wants to share it
with her foreign master
though he had shanghaied her
and had misprized her.

God chooses and uses
such collaborators
and accomplices
to bring a blessing
and hope and healing—
although we
do not approve
loving one's enemies
and doing good
to those who use us
harshly or despitefully.

II Kings 5:1-14

ONE GOOD QUALITY_____

Jezebel painting her face
has prompted the impression
that she was still primping
in casual vanity
in her last moments.
By Phoenician standards
her quick cosmetics
were a noble gesture
for death with dignity
when the call came.
She may have lived
like a hellcat
but she wanted to die
as decorously as possible.
And don't we all?

II Kings 9:30

JEZEBEL AND ATHALIAH
(Like Mother, Like Daughter)_____

They believed in conversion—
by coercion—
and salvation
by the blood—
of other people.

DOGMATIC THEOLOGY _____

Athaliah
was a malevolent
dictator.
Indoctrinated
by her mother
Jezebel
she followed
her directions
down to the last
drop of blood.

II Kings 11

HULDAH

AGITATOR?_____

Was Huldah
the prophetess
a mischief-maker
when she set
the seal of her approval
upon the stringent law
hidden so long—
so long unheeded—
and told the king
it was imperative
to break the idols
and worship
the one true God
only and always?

Or was her word
the holy impetus
her nation needed?

II Kings 22:11-14
II Chronicles 34:22

91

JONAH'S WIFE*

Jonah's wife worried
where he went
on those long trips.

A traveling salesman
with nothing in his briefcase.
What were his commissions?

What was he peddling
and for the love of God
why didn't he bring some home?

Tarshish, he told her,
Nineveh,
and one big fish story.

But better than having him
bellyaching at home
about her and her relatives.

Black sheep, he called them,
mongrels, aliens—
even his own children.

*neo-apocryphal
(not actually mentioned in the book of Jonah)

CELESTIAL CLOUDBURST _____

God's Spirit
isn't rationed
or restricted
or allotted
on the basis
of seniority
or sex
or—least of all—
fortuitous
immunity
from servitude.

God's dream
and destination
is a day
when all flesh
in all places
is sensitive
and receptive
to torrents
freshets
floods
and inundations
of the Spirit.

Joel 2:28-29

10 *After the Exile*_____

THE VALOR OF VASHTI

What else was Vashti the Queen supposed to wear
besides her jeweled turban when the King
called for her prompt appearance at the banquet
where he was celebrating his success
in sovereignty and splendor? Must she dance
in sensuous rhythms to excite the fancies
of princes, nobles, governors, and generals
who had been dining and wining seven days and nights?

When the seven trusted eunuch chamberlains
delivered the order, Vashti was not willing
and said so with a chaste and quiet candor.
Xerxes was baffled by her brash defiance
and asked his wise men how to bridge the impasse.

Memucan summarized their august views
by pointing out the plight, predicament,
and pretty pass which all men of the kingdom
would come to if their wives should ever learn
of the Queen's behavior—of her obstinacy
and her extreme unmanageability
and having a mind of her own and using it.
If he should treat her like a gentleman,
he would be opening a Pandora's box
of contempt and of wrath and willfulness
which might result in women's liberation!

So they counseled him for all their sakes
as well as his to muzzle the madcap Queen
and find another at his earliest
convenience. Thereupon Ahasuerus
(Xerxes' longer name) was pleased to oblige
and sent a solemn letter in the language
and script of every royal province
saying each man in his own house was lord
and master, boss, cock of the roost,
and any other unpretentious titles
which he might choose to fit his masculine
modesty and manifest superiority.

Queen Vashti lost her crown but not her head.
Xerxes had power to vacate her throne
but not the knack to make her hate herself
or denigrate her beautiful integrity.
He could not terminate her majesty.

Esther 1

FOR SUCH A TIME

Esther was not seduced
into forgetting her heritage
by winning the Miss Persia contest
(for which she had been drafted)
or by being awarded the throne
or by nine years of affluence
and success in secrecy and concealment
of her race and her religion.
She must have been tempted
to save her own beautiful skin
but love and loyalty were
the keys to her resistance.
Her strength was matched by her charm
and her guile by her heroism.
And at the crucial moment
she contrived to crush
the adversary of her people.

JOB'S WIFE

Job's wife is often caricatured
as a second Satan since she said
"Curse God and die," though few would like
to have their own biographies encapsuled
in one phrase in or out of context.
At least she didn't prostitute theology
and make believe to dust her husband's ashpit.

We don't know whether she brought out snacks
or started a barbecue to feed his friends
who were so hungry to devour him.

Perhaps she had to take a job
to shield herself from the poorhouse and provide
for doctor's bills—if one would come—
and to take her mind off what the patient looked like
and all that had happened to her as well as him.

Job did not cry which doesn't mean she didn't.

It's hard to have a hero for a husband.

Job 2:9-10

INTERVIEW _____

I questioned Job:
"How did you ever happen
to have such luscious daughters
as their names convey
and as your saga celebrates?
Did they take after you
in courage, eloquence, and wisdom?
What was their mother's
contribution?"

He smiled at my fatuity.

I tried again:
"Why did you choose
to bequeath a handsome share
of your considerable estate
to those whose sex
would ordinarily be
a hopeless handicap
in matters that matter
such as money
and inheritance?"

"I think"—he said—
"I have some sensibility
for what is fair."

Job 42:13-15

11 Some Conclusions

MY MOTHER

O God, my Mother,
You carried me
from conception.
You delivered me
from darkness.
You nourished me
and sustained me.
You let me crawl
and taught me to walk.
You put the first word
in my mouth.
You encouraged me.
You guided me.
You agonized
in my hurts
and my hurtfulness.
You let me go
but never stopped loving,
O God, my Mother.

Hosea 11

TRANSCENDER OF GENDER _____

Three of the Hebrew
nouns that name
and designate
the energies
of God
are feminine—
Spirit
and Wisdom
and, sometimes,
Righteousness.
This doesn't go
to remake God
into a woman
but simply
and sublimely
stresses
that the universal
Being
is the transcender
of gender
as well as
the outdistancer
of every other
attribute
which we theologize.

HIGH CALLING

Everlastingly
Yahweh
(known also
as Father
and King
and Husband)
lives by other
names and occupations
as well.
Involved so often
in doing the work
of women
we find our God
carrying water
and preparing meals.
Yes, it is Yahweh
who gives them
meat and bread
through their long
wilderness detour.
Yahweh who feeds
with wheat and butter
honey and milk
and oil and wine.
Yahweh who brings
the water from the rock
who keeps the people
clothed and like a mother
gives birth
nurses the babes
teaches the toddlers
and delights to comfort.

The Everlasting God
does not grow weary
in the satisfactions
of being Provider
and Sustainer
and loving and caring Servant
to a child-like world.

THESE WOMEN _____

It is not my purpose
to judge these people.
They judge themselves.
Their struggle
their response
illuminate
the choices
and the agonies
we face ourselves.
Decisions—
quick ones—
and the gradual
climb or decline
define their stance—
the undecreed degree
of their commitment
and staying power.
We marvel
at the quality
of their integrity
and the explosive
dialectic
of their courage
and audacity.
Given their givenness
they open poignant options
for our own
avowals.

A REAL WOMAN

A virtuous woman
is not apt
to be described
in current days
in terms of distaffs
spindles
wool
flax
willing hands—
although her hands
may be industrious
and skilled
and beautiful
and more than willing.

Setting an early alarm clock
getting her husband's breakfast
being his trusted slave
his homebound sweatshop
his unsalaried housekeeper
or even general manager
of his success
are not prerequisites—
or even having a husband.

Virtuous as she may be
she is not likely
to prize that terminology
as something presumed
prescribed
and preordained
neatly reserved
for her sex solely.

Still
as through the centuries
of worthy women
she will be clothed
with strength
and dignity
and honor.
Her hands
and heart
will feed
the poor
the needy.
Her lips
speak wisdom
and intuitive
concern
and kindness.

But she will seek
her personal destiny
do her own thing
be her own being
follow her special star
and not be satellite.

If she has children
they will call her blessed
to the degree
she gives them
space and structure
and the love
that knows when to relinquish
though still to cherish.

Her husband—
if she has one—
will praise her
for being herself
for giving and receiving
and having the courage
to choose
her style and stance—
and him!

Whatever her circumstance
tender her the credit
that she deserves
not for having been born
a woman
and having made
the best of it
but for being
a person
as much the image
of God
as any man may be.

Proverbs 31:10-31

STUDY
GUIDE _____

Suggestions for Productive Reading

Eve and After is for men and women, for young people and old, for biblical scholars, biblical neophytes, and all those in between, for those with literary inclinations as well as those who may prefer to read such poetry as though it were prose, for Jews and Christians, for clergy looking for springboards for sermons and also for laypeople who want entertaining and accurate but concise information to increase their biblical knowledge.

But *Eve and After* is first of all meant to be *enjoyed* as poetry in a biblical vein. Much of the Bible is written in poetry, and most of what is not printed as poetry is poetic in its language, its rhythm, and its imagery. In reading these poems I hope you will appreciate not only their form but their content — that you will find in them observations and insights that will help you in your daily living.

Eve and After can be used as a devotional book — though not in any stereotyped sense. Use it as a daily guide or an occasional resource to help you center on the significance of life and your response to it. See, for example, what Shiphrah and Puah — or Naomi or Ruth or Vashti — have to say to you today. And remember that these biblical women do not communicate only with their own sex; whether you are male or female, you will discover that these women have something to say to you.

Eve and After can also be used as a kind of textbook that supplements and complements the biblical passages it explores. To maximize the benefits of this kind of study, you should use at least two different translations of the Bible as well as reference books such as *The Interpreter's Dictionary* and *The Interpreter's Bible*.

To assist your study, I've prepared this simple guide. What it does is to ask a few questions for you to think about on your own or discuss with others. It also offers a few pertinent comments here and there, endeavoring to answer some of the questions that might occur to you. The guide is meant to make these poems more successful channels or vehicles of something God wants said today.

Of course, this cannot begin to be a complete commentary on the numerous women of the Old Testament. It is meant to help introduce you to — or re-acquaint you with — a surprising number of fascinating people.

HOW TO USE THIS GUIDE

A lifetime is not enough time for our study of the Bible. Even a study of *Eve and After* with its biblical references could easily take many months if pursued daily, and a year or two if pursued weekly.

You may want to work your way through these poems in a leisurely, methodical way, or you and your group may want to proceed at whatever pace the poems and the Bible set for you.

One approach would be to choose a group of the less well-known women and concentrate on them. For example, over a ten-week period you might choose to study these women in depth:

1. Hagar
2. Shiphrah and Puah
3. the women in the wilderness
4. the daughters of Zelophehad
5. the woman of Thebez, the wise woman of Tekoa, and the wise woman of Abel
6. Tamar, daughter of David
7. Abishag
8. Athaliah, Jehosheba, and Joash's nameless nurse

110

9. Huldah
10. Vashti

Or you could hold eleven sessions, one devoted to each division of the book. With the larger groups of poems you might only have time to take turns reading aloud and making brief comments on each poem. If you needed to, you could combine sections one, two, ten, and eleven, and possibly seven and eight or eight and nine.

Groups of young people and adult groups of men and women could benefit particularly from a study of this book. You might begin your first session by handing out slips of paper and having each person jot down all the names of Old Testament women that he or she can remember. Most people probably wouldn't be able to think of more than twenty on the spur of the moment. This exercise illustrates the value of this book: it highlights more than eighty Old Testament women, all of them worth knowing.

READING *EVE AND AFTER* FIRST

I would recommend first reading *Eve and After* all the way through. Since it can be read aloud in about two-and-a-half hours, you could read it to yourself in half the time. But since it is poetry you'll probably want to read more slowly than that, even though you plan to re-read it.

Another good method would be to play the cassette tapes that I have made of my readings of these poems and follow the text of the book at the same time. Most people find it helpful to both see and hear the poems; they are meant to be read aloud. Certainly you can develop your own oral interpretations of these poems. But the cassettes would at least give you an idea of how I interpret the poetry — where I pause, what I emphasize — although even my readings vary from occasion to occasion. (The tapes are available from me at 437 Lachenauer Drive, Watertown, N.Y. 13601.)

READING THE BIBLE PASSAGES

Reading *Eve and After* all the way through will give you a better idea of which Bible passages you most want to read.

111

Remember that reading the Bible aloud provides some of the same benefits as reading poetry aloud. You will observe that many of the Bible passages are poetry or very much like poetry. Just as poetry often says something in a more concise way than prose (because it seeks to distill the essence of an event or an emotion), so also the Bible often says a great deal in a few words.

YOUR OWN CREATIVE ADVENTURES

It is my hope that *Eve and After* will stimulate your creativity. It may inspire you to compose poetry of your own, or prose — an essay, a story for adults or for children, a play, or a TV script. Or you might choose to create something in pottery or needlework or music — or use volunteer or vocational work as a creative outlet. The feeling or point of a poem can be translated into an infinite number of activities; there is no limit to the ways in which your imagination can express itself.

Role-playing can be very helpful in making these poems come alive. Be Hagar, Abraham, Lot, Jezebel — the possibilities are endless. Try especially to put yourself in the place of men if you are a woman, in the place of women if you are a man.

A SPECIAL NOTE TO CLERGY PERSONS AND WORSHIP LEADERS

Through the centuries male clergy have tended to omit or to ignore most of these women, or else to make them bear the burden of blame for sins and errors. Eve and Bathsheba have often been blamed for leading men astray. Jezebel has been a natural target. Hannah has usually been praised for her obedience and self-sacrifice, but not as a dynamic person in her own right, the author of a poem (see I Samuel 2). You will find examples of a positive approach to these women in some of my monthly articles on "Poetry for the Preacher" in the following issues of *Church Management — The Clergy Journal:* April 1981; April 1982; the 1983 issues for January, April, May/June, July, August, October; and January 1984.

If you are a worship leader, focusing on one of the lesser-known women could result in a fresh and vital experience. The poems could help.

Naturally, I am not recommending omitting the men of the Bible. But don't these women deserve equal time, at least proportionate to the frequency of their inclusion in the Bible? Someday I hope to produce a book of poems about women of the New Testament; many of them have also been ignored. But here I have concentrated on women of an era about which we are likely to know even less.

Incidentally, I have already published three collections of poetry about men of the Bible: *You! Jonah!*, *Journey with Job,* and *Mistaken Identity* (poems about Jesus). I have also published a general collection of poems called *Celebration!* All of these books are currently available from me at 437 Lachenauer Drive, Watertown, N.Y. 13601.

For a number of years I have been conducting a four-day continuing education seminar on poetry at Princeton Theological Seminary, information about which may be obtained by writing 12 Library Place, Princeton, N.J. 08540.

POINTERS ON POETRY

You may be less familiar with free verse than with traditional rhymed and metrical poetry. Good free verse involves disciplines and sometimes patterns that the poet may have in mind but which may not be readily apparent to the reader.

Among the clues to watch for in this poetry are these:

The right word — The poet has endeavored to choose the best word for meaning, sound, matching with nearby words — even appearance on the printed page. One way to test the poet's choice of words is to try to substitute synonyms.

Alliteration — This involves two or more words that repeat a sound in a line of poetry or prose. The repetition may involve initial sounds (soothing songs), or consonants that begin syllables within words. Remember that alliteration is a matter of sound rather than of spelling.

Assonance — the repetition of vowel sounds in two or more words.

Onomatopoeia — the use of words that sound like their meaning.

Puns — plays on words.

Literary allusions — In the poems you will find numerous indirect references to other biblical persons and events.

Length of lines — Notice the effect that the ending of a line has, especially in free verse. That makes you pause. It gives a certain emphasis to the last word of the line. This may temporarily lead you astray, but in a constructive way. It may also add to the emphasis of the first word on the next line, which you might have missed had all the words been in one line.

Be sure to read poems *aloud* — and not just once. Ambiguity is intentional in poetry. The greater the thought, imagination, and creativity the poet can evoke in the reader, the better. Poets hope that you will think of things they did not consciously think of themselves.

Watch for continuity of metaphors and other clues that the poet is trying to give you without making it too easy. Part of the joy of poetry is what *you* discover for yourself.

Even though parts of the poems may seem to you very similar to prose, try to stay open-minded. See whether they may speak to you and whether their poetic form may help to communicate something that might have been missed in prose.

Remember also that many of the most beautiful and meaningful passages in the Bible were originally written as poetry and even in translation may be considered to be free verse.

HOW TO READ A POEM ─────────

Look first upon the pattern of the page
whether the lines repeat the ebb and flow
of constant shores or walk irregular
or march. These are important things to know.

Is there a rhyme and, if so, does it hide
or is it obvious so none can miss
its drumbeat? Does it choose to rhyme at all,
or else obliquely? Take some note of this.

Terms may not matter much but it will help
to know the creature it intends to be —
quatrain or couplet, blank verse, free, or sonnet.
It must belong to some good family.

Speak to it. Preferably, make friends with it
by reading it aloud — so you can hear
the sound of it, for sound will give it sense,
having been made to pierce your inner ear.

Taste it. Perhaps it will not please your taste
but you will never know unless you try.
It was not made to swallow at one gulp.
You miss the savor if your mouth is dry.

Look at the pictures. There are pictures there
or it is not a poem. You may see
something the poet didn't. That's all right.
Discovery is part of poetry.

And don't be satisfied to read it once.
Love at first sight is wonderful but rare.
Acquaintance weighs capacity for love.
Choice friends are found when we are most aware.

After all this, your answer may be "No."
Not every poem has a word for you.
But gold and uranium are in those mountains
waiting for your pursuit and rendezvous.

Exploring the Poems

In the poem about Emily Dickinson that prefaces this collection, I refer to her as "demure as dynamite." The two main words in this phrase seem to contradict each other — they are paradoxical. Paradox is a part of poetry and a part of life. It helps to reveal two truths where we may have been satisfied with one.

"Demure as dynamite" is a phrase I find particularly applicable to Old Testament women as well. In what ways do biblical women resemble Emily Dickinson? Were any of these women poets? (Miriam? Deborah? Hannah? Any others?)

Remember that the biblical passages frequently referred to in the collection are essential to your study. These poems in no way exhaust the possibilities of the stories. What they may do is stimulate you to write a response that develops some facet of one or more of these stories.

1. HONEST-TO-GOD PEOPLE

These first poems are intended to provide an introduction — a launching pad — for our theme. Among other points, consider the significance and implication of some of the surprising words and phrases such as "the heterogeneity of God," "the woman alive," and "unbenign neglect." Which of the people in this book are honest to God? Which ones are not? Are we?

2. IN THE BEGINNING

Observe the sexual inclusiveness of human creation in Genesis 1:27. How does this differ from Genesis 2? Is "Poet of the Universe" an appropriate metaphor for God? (Did you know that the word *poet* comes from the Greek word for "maker"?) Discuss the meaning of the term *metaphor*. How is it different from *simile?* What is a *figure of speech?*

In the poems about Eve, consider the implications of such words as "eliciting," "freed," "labored," and "consummate." The poem "Rewarding" is not literally accurate but playful. What variation does it make on the biblical story of creation? Note that while *helper* or *helpmeet* is a high compliment from a Christian point of view (see Mark 10:43), the word might better be translated as *partner.* Go back to the poem "Real People" to find some additional qualities of Eve mentioned. Do you agree that she possessed these traits?

Poetry is not always employed in a positive way. Witness the cruelty and vengeance in Lamech's poem — the first in the Bible. Do you think his wives agreed with him? Why does the biblical author mention Naamah's name but not her contribution, while he credits Lamech's male children with the contributions they made? Why is the poem called "Originals"?

Most of my poems are based closely on the Bible. Due to our lack of information on Ms. Noah, "The Admiral's Wife" invokes a flight of imagination. Do you find the poem consistent with the story? Go through the poem and note evidences of humor. Is the humor condescending toward Noah's wife, or is it supportive of her? Does the humor point up the masculine failure to give her (and her daughters-in-law) proper credit? Have you heard Noah's name pronounced "No-way"? (See the last line of the third stanza from the end.) Take time to enjoy the subtleties of this longer poem. It is a particularly good one to read aloud.

3. THE MATRIARCHS

The material on Sarah stretches from Genesis 11 to 23. Why does this make the title of the poem "First Woman" applicable? Is there good reason for expanding the name sometimes used, "The God of Abraham," to "The God of Abraham and the God of Sarah"? She is a many-faceted person. In another poem I have written: "Of Sarah and her acerbities I sing." We must recognize her problems, conflicts, and difficult choices. But we should also note the remarkable qualities ascribed to her in "Look to Sarah." Check Isaiah 51:2 for attention given to her.

"The Trial" brings Sarah into the story of the near-sacrifice of Isaac. Do you agree with its conclusion? "Sudden Thought" may make us ask ourselves whether we are thought-full enough to tell our loved ones how much we care for them.

In "The God of Seeing," can you put yourself in Hagar's place? Recently Hagar has been singled out as a prime example of the mistreatment of women in patriarchal societies, including our own. Do you agree or disagree with this evaluation? Why? Note that Hagar, though an outcast, had two theophanies (visions of God). What is meant by the last stanza of the poem? Do we have a tendency to assume that God is revealed to those of our religious or theological persuasion but not to others? In what sense is Hagar a member of the family of the faithful? Considering her two theophanies, does God limit appearances to the people who pride themselves on their own righteousness or doctrinal correctness?

What can be said on behalf of Lot's wife? How can we know when it is best to stay and when it is best to move? Do you see any parallels to nuclear destruction in this story? In George Eliot's *Silas Marner* the observation is made that in olden times there were angels who came and took people by the hand and led them away from the city of destruction; and though we see no white-winged angels now, God continues to find messengers to guide us. How does this fit with your experience? (The word *angel* comes from *messenger*.)

In colonial times there were high mortality rates due to disease (epidemics), childbirth, and frontier dangers. Many people became widowers or widows at an early age and were likely to remarry for economic as well as romantic reasons. Now, because of increased life expectancy, there are many marriages between older people who have lost their former spouses. Does the story of Keturah shed any light or offer any guidance on the subject?

The story of Isaac and Rebekah and Jacob and Esau is well known. The poem "The Night Is Dark" approaches it obliquely: it uses a great many allusions but often in an inverted way. It also employs some internal rhyme (*guile* and *while*). The intricate weave will reward you with numerous insights if you study it carefully. For example, how does Rebekah's love relate to the ladder in Jacob's dream? In what sense is that ladder a *bridge?*

Why do you suppose the biblical historian takes the space to give us two references to Rebekah's nurse, Deborah? Perhaps she was famed in ways we do not know about. Or is this a way of saying that an individual life is important even if it is not in the forefront of history? Does it applaud faithfulness? Why is it an *oak* rather than a *willow* of weeping? Where else do we hear of Bethel?

We would do well to recall the tender love story of Rachel and Jacob, although "Like Rachel" does not tell of that or of her long wait for a child. (She eventually conceived and gave birth to Joseph; she died in giving birth to her second son, Benjamin.) In the book of Jeremiah, Rachel is represented as the ancestor of the northern tribes who weeps over their defeat and exile. (The passage is quoted in Matthew 2:18.) The poem incorporates the grief of the world's mothers.

Leah has gotten "bad press." What new thoughts about Leah are provided by "In Disguise" and "Lost in the Lore"? Was it her fault that her father, Laban, deceived Jacob by giving her to Jacob as his first wife? Could she have done anything different? She became the mother of six of the twelve sons of Jacob and of a daughter, Dinah.

"Our Sister Dinah" attempts to do justice to one of the most unpleasant, violent, sensual episodes in the Old Testament. Can you see any reason for including it in the Bible — besides the fact that the Bible tells the worst as well as the best? More importantly, can you identify with Dinah? How many women's lives have been hurt by male mismanagement! (There is even a legend that Asenath, whom Joseph married in Egypt, had been adopted by the priest Potiphera and was the child of Dinah and Shechem.)

Be sure not to confuse Tamar, the daughter-in-law of Judah, with the later Tamar, daughter of David and Maachah. This is another of the strange stories of Genesis, one that explores ethics somewhat similar to the existential ethics of Lot's daughters in the Dead Sea cave following the presumed destruction of their world. This story may have been included because it recognizes the principle of the Levirate marriage, which is so important in the book of Ruth. (Perez, one of Tamar's twin sons, is included in the genealogy at the end of the book of Ruth.) Why do you think the Levirate marriage could have been a useful custom? Does it seem fair that Tamar should have faced the death penalty when Judah did not? Think of other people in the Bible who used cleverness and ingenuity and are applauded for it even though their actions were not moral or ethical in our eyes. Note in this passage the reference to Onan, and observe that his "sin" was not the nature of his sexual act but rather his unwillingness to provide a child for his brother's widow.

4. EGYPT, EXODUS, AND ENTRY

This section begins with the period, described near the end of Genesis, when Joseph entered Egypt, and covers the next five books of the Bible, including the book of Joshua.

Potiphar's wife is a glamorous figure. See especially Thomas Mann's "Joseph in Egypt" for an exciting expansion of the story. She saw nothing wrong with her attempt to capture Joseph, but she was grievously unfair in her false accusation. She saw no other alternative to protect herself. Do we ever put "survival" first? Contrast the values of Joseph with those of this woman. In Genesis 39:9 Joseph asks why he should do this great evil; he does not ask why he shouldn't do it, which is the easier approach. Joseph's story here and elsewhere illustrates again how what appears to be bad fortune may turn out to have providential results.

Asenath, the name of Joseph's Egyptian bride, may not be familiar to us. Strangely, we are not given the names of the wives of Joseph's eleven brothers. Jacob, when he came to Egypt, blessed Ephraim and Manasseh in a reverse blessing (as his father Isaac had unintentionally done) and called them his own sons. This paved the way for two of the twelve tribes of Israel to be named for them in place of Joseph. In the light of this poem, discuss priorities from the standpoint of both husband and wife. Where do you rate with your spouse? Should God come ahead of you in your spouse's dedication? Should your spouse's job — or hobby — come ahead of you?

Shiphrah and Puah were of vital importance to the Mosaic revolution and liberation, but they are usually overlooked and their names forgotten. Observe their courage, the risks they took, and their wit in their reply to Pharaoh, who at that moment seems amusingly gullible. Some scholars think that Shiphrah and Puah were Egyptian rather than Hebrew. If that is true, does this increase your admiration of them? Did it help that there were two of them instead of only one? How could they support one another? How can we support one another in good causes? Is it appropriate to call them conscientious objectors? What was their true vocation? Are they the fore-mothers of the Jewish revolution which led to the Exodus and the Promised Land? Note the phrases "floating infant," "holy orders," and "steal away." Does this last remind you of a Negro spiritual which was significant in a later escape from slavery?

Use your imagination regarding the feelings and responses of Pharaoh's daughter as the dramatic story of Moses unfolds. Do you think that she was glad she saved Moses? Does this poem offer any ideas?

We all know about Moses' mother but may not know her name — Jochebed. (She is mentioned in a later poem entitled "Not Forty Years.") We do know her daughter's name — Miriam — but may not have recognized her as being "emanci-pation's mouthpiece" or poet and administrator. Why is Miriam's song in Exodus 15 so much shorter than that of Moses? When it says that Moses sang, does that necessarily mean that Moses composed the song? Is it possible that Miriam composed both songs? Would these songs have been written down at that point in history, or do we have them because they were memorized and passed on to succeeding generations? Notice that Miriam is part of a ruling triumvirate with Moses and Aaron. Does the leprosy incident seem fair to you, especially since Aaron was equally responsible but went unpunished? When Miriam said, "Does the Lord speak only through Moses?" was that another way of asking, "Does the Lord speak only through men?"

Did you know the name of Moses' wife? Read the romantic account of how she met Moses and became his wife. What complicated life for her? Whose "fault" was it?

Read the two passages about the women in the wilderness and also the parallel passages in which the women are not even mentioned. Why do you think they were omitted the first time? If it was so easy to overlook these women, does it suggest the likelihood that women played a much greater part in events than the history records? What other groups have been omitted in our history books? Discuss how we today — both women and men — can use our skills in God's service. Should it be only women who are unpaid volunteers? Should they always be an "auxiliary" instead of "the real thing"? Give as many examples of skills used in God's service as you can. We tend to discount or ignore the gifts of people whom we consider different or less important. Does God do the same?

Think about the implications of "Last Laugh." Can you justify this downgrading of women in Levitical law? Are there other Levitical laws which have been superseded? What is your favorite verse in Leviticus? See Leviticus 19. Read the whole chapter, but note especially verse 18.

"The Daughters of Zelophehad" is written as a ballad. What were the qualities of these five women? What do you notice about how easy it was to ignore the rights of women? Was Moses' first ruling fair or merely an improvement on the previous situation? How human is it for people to find or demand loopholes? What connection does the action of the daughters of Zelophehad have with the fact that Elizabeth II became sovereign?

Rahab is the star of the well-known Battle of Jericho. Was she justified in betraying her country? Was she what we would call a defector? (We approve a person's defection to our side!) What other harlots besides Rahab are mentioned in the Bible? Do you think that Christians made a point of including her in the New Testament because she was (1) an ancestor of Jesus? (2) an outstanding example of faith? (3) an outstanding example of good works? It is possible that she was actually an innkeeper. Does that change your feelings about her?

5. IN THE DAYS OF THE JUDGES

"A Tale of Three Women" gives us insight into the characters of three very different people. Since Sisera's mother is the "speaker" in the poem — the story is told from her point of view — does this increase your sympathy for her? your understanding of her feeling as to how war brings grief to both sides? Deborah is certainly the most appealing judge in the book of Judges. She must have been a remarkable woman. List her many talents. Note that as judge she was both a personal counselor and a legal authority. Do you see appropriate reasons for her name meaning "bee" and Barak's meaning "lightning"? Discuss the words of Judges 5:20. Does Jael make a good role model? The poem (it *is* a poem) in Judges 5 must have been composed much earlier than the prose account in Judges 4. We are grateful for the parallel stories.

Are you surprised at the woman of Thebez? Though we know it is wrong to kill even one person, we cannot help admiring her decisive and spectacular remedy. Faced with her city's destruction by Abimilech, who had set himself up as king, she used her head — or rather, his! One of seventy sons of Gideon (Jerubbaal), he was trying to cash in on his father's fame, and proceeded to dispatch all of his brothers except Jotham, who did not want to be king anyway (see his famous parable in Judges 9:8-15). This story from the barbarous days of the Judges shows how one woman succeeded in bringing about peace. Does she offer us any clues for peace-making? I think she does. What about the humor of Abimilech's embarrassment at being mortally wounded by a woman? Obviously the millstone was not a one-ton stone from a grinding mill but her home grinding stone — the smaller upper one. Still, it was heavy enough to "ground" the tyrant.

Jephthah's unnecessary and unjust vow results in a story both absurd and gruesome. If his daughter had been a son, or if his vow had turned on himself, he would very likely have found a way around it. See I Samuel 14:43-45 and the account which precedes it. What other rash vows do you recall — including your own? Should Jephthah's daughter have rebelled against her father's vow instead of being so acquiescent? Does the story indicate that Jephthah was more concerned with his own feelings than his daughter's? Is there an indication that Jephthah's daughter was ritually important to the women of Israel for a long time afterwards? Does war involve vowing to sacrifice a part of our people — especially the young? Are there other ways we sacrifice our children? In another poem on this same theme I have concluded:

We need commitment now
not at the cost
of someone else
but of ourselves.

As you recall Samson's "comical adventures," you discover that, while five women are mentioned, he seems to have had little regard for any of them. His mother is a spiritual and heroic person whose theophanies (visions of God) are significant. Her dedication and devotion seem to have gone for naught, except that she provided her people with a memorable — but not "religious" — folk hero whose stupidities exceed even his strength. Observe the elements of humor, of hyperbole, of cleverness, of inanity, of inhumanity. Somehow we can't help enjoying these stories, and we will never forget Samson, or Delilah with "her dazzle and her fireworks," as I have described her in another poem. See also "Not Like Delilah" in the section of poems about Ruth.

Another almost unbelievable and gruesome story is that of the Levite's concubine, whom we might also call the Levite's wife. It involves violent sex, senseless sex, and senseless violence. What does it reveal about the treatment of women? Does it give us any guidance regarding "law and order"? How much grief is caused in our world by man's inhumanity to man and woman's to woman and the combination of both? Is all this related to genocide and holocaust?

6. THE ROMANCE OF RUTH

Read the book of Ruth — preferably aloud. Just enjoy it; it doesn't have to "say something" to you — but it will. How do you think it happened to get into the Bible? Can you imagine, as some scholars believe, that the tale was originally written in poetry and that the prose version was written some time later? Read all of the poems in this section and see how they fit with the biblical story. You will need to discover for yourself where each individual poem is relevant in the following comments and questions.

Is the story of Ruth sentimental or matter-of-fact? tender or tough? realistic or romantic? In what ways is this book similar to the book of Jonah? to the book of Esther? to the Song of

Solomon? Do you think the author had any political or socio-logical or theological motives in writing this story? Outline the "plot" of the story of Ruth. Do you find suspense? In what ways is it like an historical novel? Who are the heroes or heroines? What villains do you observe? Is there much dia-logue? How does the author communicate details? Would you call him (or her) verbose? Does he (or she) employ humor, wit, irony? Is there any point at which the author or reader might smile or have a twinkle in the eye? Do you recognize an appreciation of the clever actions of any of the characters?

In reading poems, plays, novels, and literature in general, part of the significance for us is the opportunity to identify with other people and learn about their feelings and points of view. Examine the relationships of the people in the story. What persons are you most like? Which one would you most like to be? Watch for everyday human touches. Do you find any evidence of conflict? Where do you find evidence of cooperation? We inevitably compare people, though not al-ways in a kindly spirit. In as kindly a spirit as possible, com-pare Ruth first with Orpah and then with Naomi. Compare the attitude of Boaz with the possible attitude of others in his position in the community and with that of the "near kins-man." Compare Ruth and Boaz. What about Orpah? Does "How Easily a Love Aborts" shed a different light on her? After all, she did show love to Naomi as well as loyalty to her own mother and nation; there is nothing blameworthy in her actions. How do you feel about Naomi? Is she devoted, selfish, or somewhere in between? Is she the most important charac-ter in the book? Consider the different ideas about Naomi expressed in the poems about her. Do we learn more about these people by what they say or by what they do? How do people learn about us?

The story depicts people in difficult, fragile, potentially fruitful everyday relationships. Reflect on the relationships between husband and wife (four pairs in this brief book); in-laws (how many such relationships do you find?); neigh-bors; fellow workers; foreigners; old and young; rich and poor. Consider the feelings of a person who goes to a new home, especially at a great distance from his or her homeland. Have you done this? Do you have neighbors who have? How does one feel in a new job? What prompts people to move? What prompted Elimilech and Naomi to move to Moab? What caused Naomi to return to Israel?

A crucial problem today (and always) is race relations. How was Elimilech's family treated in Moab? How was Ruth treated in Bethlehem? Why might Ruth have been more "acceptable" than other foreigners?

In what ways did Ruth exercise her civil rights? Do you feel that she was a full person rather than one defined primarily in terms of her sex? Why? How do you think she would react in a similar situation in today's world? What do you think of Ruth's proposal to Boaz? Does it remind you of our "turnaround" tradition of Leap Year? Will increasing women's rights affect romance?

What does the story say, directly or indirectly, about hunger, famine, unemployment? What are you and your church doing to alleviate these problems and to find solutions? Some communities have a very effective urban mission or similar organization. (One is in Watertown, N.Y.)

What do you gather about the inclusion of the genealogy? Read also Matthew 1:1-6 or even 1-17. In what ways do we have a right to be proud of ancestors? What about people who find themselves in circumstances which force them to become the "roots" for later generations when their own "roots" are either unknown or totally unsatisfactory? Identify the great-grandmother and the great-grandson in the imaginative poem "Great-grandmother." Do you think this possibly could have happened?

Ruth does not seem to be a "religious" book. Are there ways in which this might be an advantage? How do we define *religious?* Is this word sometimes a stumbling block? Do you think we should divide the world into religious and secular spheres? Do God's Word and will apply to all aspects of life? What evidence of worship or cult do you find in the book of Ruth? How often does God's name appear, and in what connection? Does the author take for granted the religious heritage of Israel? We often speak of being *good.* What ideas of *goodness* do you find in this book? Is situational ethics involved in this story? See "Not Like Delilah," "Proposal," and the earlier poem "God Was Not Shocked." The book of Ruth is concerned with everyday life. Is this where our service to God is rendered? Give examples of how this story stresses the significance of the happenings of our common days and of ordinary people. Are responsibility, obligation, obedience, and sacrifice essential to human life? What about mercy and compassion?

What quality do Ruth and Boaz have most in common? In what ways might the book of Ruth help us to be more compassionate? Sympathy and admiration are excellent qualities. Suppose Boaz had restricted his feelings for Ruth to sympathy and admiration?

The book of Ruth may be read as a commentary on the problem of suffering. It also suggests the idea of God as shelter (2:12). Can human beings provide God's shelter for others? How? Another idea of God — only hinted at — is that of Redeemer. The Hebrew word is *go-el*. Look for the idea in chapters 3 and 4.

The story of Ruth tells us that God works in the seemingly small events of everyday life, not necessarily in the spectacular or miraculous events. Even "belittled Bethlehem" is a place where God is at work. What do Bethlehem and Nazareth have in common? In Ruth's story we find an eloquent account of the purposes of God affecting a life that surely at first gave no evidence of being any more significant than we may think our own lives to be. Whether we be adults or youths, female or male, poor or rich, faced with happy or unhappy prospects, we can identify with Ruth as well as with others in her story. How much more does it mean to you now?

7. THE BEGINNINGS OF MONARCHY

Do you see any parallel between Hannah's willingness to part with Samuel and Abraham's readiness to sacrifice Isaac? Are there times when distraught people are unjustly accused of drunkenness or drug use? Hannah is one of the relatively few Old Testament women who have been frequently praised by preachers. Why? Are you satisfied with the reasons? Do you find any qualities in Hannah in addition to subservience and obedience? Note that "Anna" is another form of "Hannah." Are the questions Elkanah asks Hannah (in I Samuel 1:8) another way of telling her "I love you"? Note the following chapter. In another poem I said of Hannah,

> And Hannah sang
> in answer
> to God's answer.

Do you see any parallels with the Magnificat in Luke 1? What other stories of birth are important in the Bible?

Peninnah (remember her?) does not come across as a likeable person. Do we? In a culture which prized children (especially sons!) above all else, Peninnah was fortunate to have so many children. Hannah, the other wife (permissible in those days), languished in barrenness and felt it to be a sign of God's displeasure. Do we ever gloat over our good fortune? Do we take it to be proof of our excellence or our favor with God? In what ways could Peninnah have been more considerate? I once described Peninnah's insensitivity this way:

> She tried to put Hannah
> in her place
> instead of trying
> to put herself in Hannah's.

There are times in history when the future looks bleak for everyone, especially for those whose own family has failed or betrayed them. The wife of Phinehas (who was one of Eli's disappointing sons) lost both her devout father-in-law and her reprobate husband at the time that the sacred ark was captured. About to bear a fatherless child, life seemed too much for her, a feeling which may have contributed to her death. Would you name a child Ichabod? Do you suppose people once named sons Ichabod without realizing the significance of the name? Is there anything that causes God's glory to disappear or be dimmed? Do we contribute to such a situation?

David had eight wives. The first was Michal, but she is not necessarily the best known, although the Bible tells us quite a bit about her. Michal was the daughter of Saul and Ahinoam and the sister of Jonathan and Merab. Like Jonathan, she had to decide whether Saul or David had the primary claim to her loyalty. Are we ever faced with such choices? Michal's love affair with David was beautiful and romantic. Most marriages start that way, but the events of life get complicated. Trace Michal's story to discover the ups and downs of happiness. Do you feel she was treated unjustly by Saul? How do you evaluate her ability to cope? Was she justified in criticizing David's dancing? Would there have been a more diplomatic way to do it? In a poem called "At the Last," I wrote:

> Twice lucky in love
> but at the last
> doomed by the truth
> she let her lips
> declare.

Abigail is a noteworthy person in her own right. Some women named Abigail may not be familiar with her story. ("Gail" is a shortening of her name, and "Abby" the common nickname.) Contrast the character of Abigail with that of her husband, Nabal. Are spouses sometimes faced with the problem of how to deal with different sets of values? Would you say the story has a happy ending?

The medium of Endor is often referred to as a witch. Witchcraft continues to fascinate many people. Does this poem help us see her humane qualities? Of what does "eat and be thankful" remind you? A few lines from another poem I wrote about her pay her this compliment:

> She was a good witch
> if there ever was one.

Bathsheba is the best known of David's wives, and was presumably the most beautiful. Hollywood produced a movie about her and David. As a woman, was she treated like a piece of property? Did the king, as absolute monarch, have a right to treat her as his property also? We certainly do not see David at his best in this first episode, nor in his dispatching of Uriah, one of the most despicable acts of his life. How would you characterize Bathsheba in her efforts to make her son Solomon heir to the throne?

Discover for yourself again how marvelously the tragic story of Tamar (daughter of David and Maachah) is told in II Samuel 13. Writing a poem about her experience proved to be the most difficult challenge of this collection. I wrote a ballad, trying to make it bearable, but that poem could have been mistaken as a lighthearted approach. It ended with these lines:

> And Tamars still, no matter how good,
> may be ostracized and misunderstood.

After several other attempts, I thought of telling the story from the standpoint of the person least likely to tell it: Jonadab, Amnon's cousin and friend. Perhaps I have imbued him with too much understanding and too much sensitivity; you can decide. This moving episode involves both rape and incest. How are victims of both these crimes likely to be treated today? What about the misuse of God's gift of sex? Was Amnon selfish as well as sex-obsessed? Was Tamar's brother Absalom less interested in how his sister felt than in what Amnon's sin could do for him in becoming king? An interesting footnote is that Absalom named his own daughter Tamar.

Discuss the story of the wise woman of Tekoa in depth. Old Testament parables differ in many ways from those of Jesus. Is there any parallel here to Jesus' story of the prodigal son? Do the fathers react similarly? Since David only partially forgave Absalom, it led to Absalom's bitterness toward his father, which led to his tragic rebellion, a civil war, and his death. Where have you heard of Tekoa before? The wise woman of Tekoa was a peacemaker, showing initiative and creativity in handling a problem which not only threatened civil war for her country but vexed the spirit of her king. Was she a true ambassador of reconciliation? See II Corinthians 5:19-20. While the historian gives Joab the major credit for her felicitous wording, I believe that this woman should be given the praise and honor. In telling her parable she uses some of the saddest and most beautiful words ever spoken or written (II Samuel 14:14). They are reason enough for our trying to get along in our world without bloodshed. God provides us with many parables which we could interpret in a broader sense as guides for reconciled living. See the poem "God's Parables."

> When it comes down
> to skilled negotiation

to save a city
the eminently wise
woman of Abel
deserves much more
than honorable mention.

So began a much longer poem about this "Percipient Peace-maker." Does she deserve the title of "wise woman"? It indicates that she had already won a reputation for sagacity and leadership. Notice that Joab had not even told the people of Abel why he was attacking their city. Can you think of similar stupidities in the history of human warfare? Would you call this woman a peacemaker? Would you call her the savior of her city? Would we have found a more humane way of delivering Sheba, the son of Bichri, the Benjaminite trying to usurp David's throne, to Joab? Do you approve of Joab's search and destroy methods? Is such "pacification" still employed? Are there sometimes more options available than we take time or thought to recognize? The point to stress here is that the wise woman of Abel took the initiative to negotiate when all seemed lost. In your life, do you find a frequent need to negotiate — where you go on the family vacation, whether you buy a new car or a new freezer, whether to interchange yard equipment with your neighbor, etc.

In considering Rizpah's excruciating story, I have chosen to emphasize her "steadfast love." This is one of the English translations of the tremendously meaningful Hebrew word *hesed*. Does Rizpah's love remind you at all of God's love? How? Look in a volume of the collected poetry of Alfred Lord Tennyson for a long and moving poem entitled "Rizpah."

Read the two poems about Abishag. They are written as dramatic monologues — one features David speaking, the other, Abishag. Either poem might have been titled "What the Doctor Ordered." David's doctors and/or his counselors wanted to remain in power. They recommended this expedient to keep David warm — and alive! — which would be difficult without "central heating." It also relates to the belief of neighboring nations that a king could not continue to rule once he lost his sexual potency. Does either poem arouse our empathy for a person who has grown old? for one who is young and inexperienced and homesick? Is there any similarity here between David and Shakespeare's King Lear? Do you find a reference to the Twenty-third Psalm?

A poem I wrote called "Who Then Is Wise?" begins,

> Solomon's wisdom
> gets top billing
> in the "Which is
> the real mother?"
> conundrum.

This well-known story is usually used to demonstrate and illustrate Solomon's proverbial wisdom. As in our response to many Bible stories, in our response to this story we have tended to emphasize one person at the expense of others who are treated as minor characters with no importance of their own. After reading these two poems, try identifying first with the real mother and then with the one whose child was dead. Which is easier to do? Does this approach bring *us* into the story more personally? Are we ever like either woman? How do we treat such women? Do they have a chance in our society? Is our society at all responsible for pushing them into this means of earning a living? Can Christian love do things by halves?

Everyone has heard of the Queen of Sheba — but no one knows her name. This is true of far too many biblical women. Her visit to Solomon has been celebrated by great artists. We get a "kick" out of it. Why? Does the poem offer any reasons? How do her intelligence and authority compare with those of Solomon?

8. PRAISE, LOVE, AND WISDOM

This section is an interlude inspired by two biblical books of poetry (the Psalms and the Song of Solomon — known also as the Song of Songs or Canticles), and one printed as poetry (Proverbs). How often are women mentioned in the Psalms? Explore that. They certainly sang the Psalms at various times, including on their travels to Jerusalem. In Proverbs we find more warnings against women in behalf of men than we find praise; the exception is the last chapter, which is represented in the last poem in this book. Among the negative references in Proverbs are these: 2:16-19; 5:3-6; 6:24.; 9:13; 11:22; 19:13; 21:9, 19; 25:24; 27:15. What's sauce for the gander should be sauce for the goose. But it doesn't seem to be.

In the Song of Solomon the woman takes the initiative as often as, if not more often than, the man. These love songs have been appropriated as significant allegories of God's love for his bride, Israel, or Christ's love for his bride, the Church. But basically they are a collection of love songs — with beautiful and amorous imagery from which my poems occasionally borrow not only here but in several of the poems about Ruth. Be sure to read this entire book. Are you glad it is included in the Bible? In wedding ceremonies the husband was often referred to as the king. Did it add to the popularity — and the canonicity — of the book to have Solomon's name used in its title? Do you find it appropriate to use passages from this book in a wedding now? (My poem "Rise Up, My Love, My Fair One" has been set to music by Dr. Frackenpohl and has been sung at weddings as well as used as a choir anthem.)

9. NORTH AND SOUTH

The widow of Zarephath was a helpless person who proved to be of great help to the prophet Elijah. Make your own definition of *miracle*. But do not let the questions regarding miracles obscure the joy of what happens and the joy of thanking God. If *miracles* happen in our lives, what responsibility does this place on us? Is it "safe" to share the little we may have? How much have we personally received from people who have little of this world's goods? Someone says that givers are winners. Do you believe this to be true? In what ways? What is the biblical attitude toward widows? What was the economic status of widows? Are things better today?

The unnamed prophet's unnamed widow is involved in another *miracle*. It is a delightful story. Can't you just picture it? — her going to her neighbors and borrowing all the containers she can! The possibility that she had become bankrupt because of her generosity adds to the depth of the story. The prominent Jewish historian Josephus, in his *Antiquities* (see IX.4.2.) links her story with the prophets, mentioned in I Kings 18:4, who had been faithful. The title of this poem draws on Isaiah 61:3.

In "Collaborator" we recognize that the little slave girl, who served Naaman and his wife, had been treated unjustly by being taken into captivity. But she responded — as God does — with loving-kindness. In reading this poem, pause to consider additional meanings to such words as "employs," "latitude," "misprized," "collaborator," and "accomplice." What about the irony in the last six lines? Are Jesus' words in the Sermon on the Mount taken seriously by Christians?

My poem "The Woman of Shunem" (II Kings 4:8-37) was too long and diffuse for the book. It closes with these lines:

> He lives! He lives!
> The youngster lives.
> Elisha gives him
> back to his mother.
> The miracle of restoration
> songs of rejoicing
> fill the delivered home.
>
> He lives! He lives!
>
> And God in heaven be praised —
> God who does all things well.
> He lives. He lives.

Not all the women of the Bible are admirable characters from our point of view. Jezebel ranks as one of the worst, partly due to her pagan upbringing but also due to her virulence and malevolence. Can you think of any positive characteristics that she has? Do you agree with the caveat of "One Good Quality"?

Her daughter Athaliah is another strong and cruel character. Jezebel was only the king's wife, but Athaliah took over the throne as full monarch after her husband died. In another poem I have said,

> She out-Jezebeled her mother
> and out-Heroded that later
> malignant monarch.

It is interesting that we often find "bad" people more exciting than "good" people. Why? Fortunately, there are two really "good" women who tried to counteract Athaliah's wickedness and succeeded. We do not know about Joash's mother but we do know that his aunt Jehosheba and his nameless nurse are heroic figures who hid him until he could take over the throne in a coup.

Huldah is a "giant" (in the best sense of the word) among biblical women. She rarely receives proper credit. She is a prophet in the prophetic tradition. Of all the people in the land, she was the one called upon to authenticate the scrolls found in the Temple,

> because of her fidelity
> to God and her capacity
> for recognizing
> the authentic
> impact of God's word.

Dr. Arlene Swidler and Dr. Leonard Swidler call her "the Founder of Biblical Studies." How do we ourselves go about verifying God's word as it comes to us in the Bible and in other ways? Are prophets sometimes treated as "mischief-makers"?

In this book Jonah's wife is the only person who is a product of the author's imagination. This poem appeared in *The New York Times* and in one of my earlier collections of poetry, *You! Jonah!* Try reading the first three stanzas of the poem and stopping there. Might this constitute a poem by itself? Dissect stanza 3 and see how it fits with the book of Jonah. Continuing with stanzas 4, 5, and 6, consider the implication of the suggestion that Jonah's own children are not pure-blooded Jews. Might this account psychologically for Jonah's attitude toward the heathen, whom he thought God should not love?

Joel 2:28-29 is the basis of "Celestial Cloudburst." You will recall it is also quoted by Peter in Acts 2. The poem is written intentionally in very short lines. Stop at the end of each line as though it was the end of the poem. Does this reading help give you additional insights? How does this passage in Joel relate to your attitudes and actions? How *inclusive* does this passage in Joel call upon us to be?

10. AFTER THE EXILE

Vashti is one of the great women in the Bible. She has been

overlooked and even denigrated and vilified. Some people have felt that she was rude to the king. But re-read the first chapter of Esther. Seven days and seven nights of alcoholic orgy preceded the issuing of her husband's request that she appear at the banquet. This was not a good time for her to be "displayed." She may have been protecting her handmaidens also. Do the details of the poem conform to the details of the first chapter of Esther? Where do you find humor in the story? Refresh your memory of the mythical story of Pandora's box (mentioned in the poem) and see how there is more than a casual connection between the two stories. Spend some time on the last stanza of the poem. Note the plays on words in the summary of Vashti's significance. Do we want to be like her? In what ways?

Esther is one of the two women for whom biblical books are named. Both books are masterpieces of storytelling and are often studied as such. Strangely, the name God does not appear in this book. It is used by the Jewish people in connection with the celebration of the Feast of Purim, as it is the basis for the feast. You may want to compare Esther with Vashti to determine their similarities and differences. Did Esther take risks? show cleverness? act decisively? The book has blood-thirsty elements and its own aspects of genocide and holocaust on both sides. Note that *Esther* means "star" and is sometimes associated with the name of a pagan goddess, Astarte. (Esther's Uncle Mordecai has a name resembling that of the pagan god Marduk). Read Esther's story as an exciting tale beautifully told. The concluding stanza of a long poem of mine telling the whole story of Esther (Hadassah) in detail says:

> Esther continued
> star of the King's heart
> sharing that spirit
> which makes a man
> or woman great and good.
> And Mordecai
> was second only
> to his sovereign
> and served the nation
> and the people of God

dedicated to their welfare
and the reign of peace —
the Lord's shalom.

Read Job 1 and 2 and see what picture you get of Job's wife. Is it fair to categorize her on the basis of so little information? The book of Job is a tremendous piece of literature and worthy of your most perceptive attention. The poetry in itself is marvelous. It is a fascinating consideration of the ways in which God deals with us and the place of suffering and mystery in life. (See my book *Journey with Job.*) The great poet and artist William Blake felt that Job's wife was a great influence for good. As you read the poem "Job's Wife," does it make you empathize with her? Her biblical words are completely logical in the light of what had been her husband's theology. What other biblical wives found it "hard to have a hero for a husband"? What biblical husbands may have found it hard to have a wife who was a national hero? In our times, do the successful careers of wives ever make their husbands feel uncomfortable or threatened?

Although the book of Job seems to ignore women's interests as such, it is actually a book for and about Everyman *and* Everywoman, and therefore Everyperson. In the last chapter we find a surprising and equitable action whereby Job treats each of his three daughters as equal to each of his seven sons in the inheritance. How about that! Look up the meanings of the daughters' names. In the concluding stanza of the poem, be sure you recognize the double meaning of the word *fair*.

11. SOME CONCLUSIONS

"My Mother" proceeds on the assumption that Hosea 11 describes the motherly attributes of God. Some scholars do not agree but insist they refer to a father. If so, as I have written elsewhere,

God must be
like a motherly father
or a fatherly mother.

In the book of Hosea we are not positive whether the

extramarital activities of the prophet's wife, Gomer, are to be taken as allegory or as actual occurrence. In either case, Hosea's love for her is a dramatic portrayal of the limitless love of God. (See my poem "Limitation" on page 39 of *You! Jonah!* This poem has since been revised to use inclusive language.)

Conclusive evidence for the gender of certain of God's attributes is not provided by the fact that the Hebrew nouns for "Spirit," "Wisdom," and — sometimes — "Righteousness" may be feminine, nor by the fact that the Latin word for farmer, *agricola,* is feminine. But they do point out that God is the Transcender of Gender and goes far beyond our highest thought.

"High Calling" refers to so many biblical passages that even a concordance would not give us all the pertinent information. One of the passages that is very illuminating for us is to be found where we might least expect it and is written in poetry — Deuteronomy 32. Unfortunately, some translators do not make it clear that God is compared with a *mother* eagle, and that God is the God who fathers and mothers us and who brings us forth in pain as a mother would. See especially verses 10, 11, and 18.

"A Real Woman" relates to Proverbs 31. That chapter indicates that biblical women could be involved in many activities — more than we ordinarily realize. Read the chapter. Does the husband get the credit for what his wife does? Does she? My poem attempts to update the chapter in the light of God's revelations. Do you agree or disagree with my deductions and observations? Think about them and see how you might change them.

In *Eve and After* it has not been my purpose to glorify biblical women unduly or to ignore their sins and mistakes and human frailties. What I have tried to do is to give them equitable consideration in a way they have too often been denied. "Invitation to Obedience," among the poems about Eve, stresses this, as does the penultimate poem, "These Women." I have tried to put myself in the place of each woman — as much as my degree of empathy will permit. I have tried to suggest strengths which have been overlooked as well as alternative interpretations of motives and events. I am indebted to many scholars and especially to Phyllis Trible and her seminal book, *God and the Rhetoric of Sexuality*. I have pondered these women as "Real People" (the title of the second poem in this book), similar in many ways to the people of our own time. I expected to find some hidden treasure; I have been rewarded with an abundance of it. The Bible does indeed speak to us today if we have "ears to hear" and "hearts to obey."